YOUR CASTABLE TYPES®

UNDERSTANDING HOW THE INDUSTRY
PERCEIVES YOUR TALENT
WILL MAXIMIZE YOUR ACTING SUCCESS

Cynthia White

YOUR CASTABLE TYPES®

*UNDERSTANDING HOW THE INDUSTRY
PERCEIVES YOUR TALENT
WILL MAXIMIZE YOUR ACTING SUCCESS*

Cynthia White

SMITH AND KRAUS PUBLISHERS   2013

ISBN: 1-57525-788-2
ISBN: 978-1-57525-788-4
Library of Congress Control Number: 2012950721

Typesetting and layout by Elizabeth E. Monteleone

A Smith and Kraus book
177 Lyme Road, Hanover, NH 03755
Editorial 603.643.6431 To Order 1.800.558.2846
www.smithandkraus.com

Printed in the United States of America

ACKNOWLEDGMENTS

My sincerest thanks to Natasha Graf and Janet Rosen for their support and guidance in bringing this book to life; to the three amazing women who shared their knowledge and mentorship with me during the most formative years of my training, Penny Allen, Mariana Hill and Anna Strasberg; to the dedicated and fearless actors who look to *me* for training and mentorship. Your talent and energy renews mine each and every day.

For Emma and Jamie with love

CONTENTS

INTRODUCTION

I KNOW WHAT YOU'RE THINKING.

It wasn't supposed to be this hard, was it? You knew an acting career would be difficult, fraught with rejection and periods of struggle. You knew you'd probably have to wait tables or take temp jobs but you were okay with that because you would be pursuing your dream, and working as an actor is the only dream you've ever had. You just didn't know how hard it would be to simply get a toe-hold in the industry, let alone succeed.

But it is.

It's harder than you imagined it would be and in ways you never could have realized. It's much, much harder than the career paths your friends follow with accessible, well defined steps to working up the career ladder in fields where they use words like benefits and payday. Those friends had help from advisors, mentors to grease the wheels and internships to get them started. No one mentored you and your acting aspirations. People actually advised you against what you wanted to do most and made you feel foolish, self-destructive even, for your choice. There weren't any acting internships to put on your resume. You scrambled to figure out how to get an agent to simply look at your headshot, once you spent every penny you had or every penny your parents lent you, on having it taken. You tried to join acting unions that can only be joined once you're hired for a union gig which you only get if you're already a member of the union only to find out how much less union work there is out there. You worked in crummy conditions for no pay or, worse yet, paid to be in a crummy showcase, just so the industry could see you in something crummy and maybe hire you for something better. All while you watched your friends with "real jobs" start to move up the ladder and cash those paychecks that come like clockwork every two weeks, with benefits and paid vacations, and you felt like crap.

It's Not Your Fault, Really.

No career is a guaranteed easy path to success or guaranteed to bring a lifetime of security. Acting can be a wonderfully creative, fulfilling and sometimes lucrative career. It can grow as you do and branch out into many other opportunities. The problem is no one will tell you how to attain your creative goals, establish yourself as a credible artist and unlock the secret of a successful acting career. Instead, schools and family and the managers and advisors you meet at the formative stages of your career guide aspiring actors in the wrong direction, sending you down a path of predictable trials and errors, chipping away at your creative, financial and emotional capital until you feel used and hopeless about ever realizing your dreams. I've not only experienced this myself as an actor but see it play out over and over as a coach, producer and director. The quicksand and land mines that derail careers and ambush talent are so time worn and inevitable that I think of them like a syndrome that needs to be cured. When you recognize that everyone is vulnerable to these traps, my hope is you'll feel less like a uniquely singled out idiot actor and more like a person who has yet to receive the guidance their talent and drive deserve.

I have always been of the opinion that there is not enough art in the world nor support and encouragement for those who create it. When I started my coaching consultancy in 1999, after years of working as an actor, director and producer, my goal was, and continues to be, to empower actors to realize their creative goals fully, making use of their wide ranging abilities. This guiding principle was born out of the knowledge that so many wonderful actors never have the chance to share their talents because they are forced to chase after careers as opposed to creating them.

Designed to guide actors to take charge of their careers creatively and professionally, my approach to acting training is accessible, offering a blueprint for achieving acting goals and navigating the realities of the business while cultivating artistic talent and an understanding of the industry. I hope that you, like my private clients, will enjoy the confidence and results the Castable Types® Approach can bring to your acting career. It is a great source of joy to me to help fellow actors turn their passion into a profession. With the right technique and a clearer understanding of how your talent is viewed by agents and casting directors, your acting career can become a reality.

PART I:

UNDERSTANDING YOUR CASTABLE TYPES®

CHAPTER 1

YOUR CASTABLE TYPES:
HOW THE INDUSTRY PERCEIVES YOU

IF *HE* GETS IT....

A few years ago I found myself engaged in a phone conversation with a friendly, helpful man from the United States Patent and Trademark Office named Wilbur. We were discussing acting. I had submitted an application to trademark Castable Types as it had become a core component of my work as a professional acting and career coach. Wilbur, who was reviewing my application, had a few questions. Now, you might think the last person in the world who would understand anything about acting, casting and the industry would be found sitting in a cubicle at the United States Patent and Trademark office, but you would be wrong.

"Can you give me an example of how you use Castable Types in a coaching session?" he asked. I was happy to oblige.

"I had a new client come to me for coaching. I asked her what type of roles she is called in to read for and what are the parts she books most. The client said she gets called in for all kinds of roles although she doesn't book very many. She could play anything from 18 to 30, dramatic, comedic, upscale, downscale. It didn't matter, she said, as long as she could look the part, she could do it. She could stretch. She had range"

"Isn't that the way actors are supposed to go at it?" asked Wilbur.

"Not if they want to book work" I replied. "Casting directors aren't looking for stretch. They're looking for a terrific actor who *is* the part. Someone who can embody it physically, inhabit it emotionally, connect to it more fully and authentically than the other actors at the audition."

Wilbur paused for a moment and then said, "So appearance doesn't matter for actors anymore."

"Of course it does" I answered, "but not in the way most actors believe".

I then explained that my client was a fit, vibrant woman in her late 20's. If you saw her in a photo, you could reasonably take her for a college junior or senior. But once you saw her move or heard her speak, you would immediately know she was an independent adult who had been making her way in the world for a number of years. You could pick up her determined, knowing nature, which came from the life experience she had gained over the last decade. She was buoyant and bubbly to be sure, but definitely not a kid. If she was reading for the role of a college coed, she could look the part but as soon as she spoke, you would know in an instant she was all wrong for the role. Not a bad actor, just wrong for the role. If the other actors at the audition were between 20 and 24, you would pick up on the difference just from her energy and body language. So her casual, youthful, appearance was out of line with her Castable Type. It would be much easier to bring her look in line with her Castable Type then for her to squelch the essential elements of her personality and spirit so she could try to play younger, less grounded and mature roles. Doing that would make her un-castable. Her bubbly personality was better suited to being excited at the idea of becoming a parent, buying a home or getting a promotion, not spring break. She would never be the actor who embodies the role and brings it to life with authenticity. She would lose the edge a clearly defined, organic, recognizable identity gives an actor and diminish her chances of booking work.

"So," I told Wilbur, "I taught this client how to understand, define and use her Castable Types to bring more of her unique qualities and energy to her acting, making her more connected and alive in roles. We worked to bring her look in line with her Castable Types. We then created a career plan of action with achievable goals in areas of the industry where her Castable Type is in demand. This career makeover significantly raised her ability to get representation and professional auditions which re-energized her focus and commitment to acting. that, in turn, allowed me to raise her acting technique to a far more nuanced performance level, strengthening her ability to succeed in the casting process and book jobs."

"I get it." He said. "Your trademark is approved."

❑❐❑❐

If an examiner from a government cube farm understands the wisdom, value, creative and competitive edge an actor gets from a Castable Types® approach to acting and career development, you should, too. Because, in the eyes of the industry and Wilbur, you are your Castable Types.

EMBRACING YOUR CASTABLE TYPES

If you think of your career as a small business, your Castable Types are your unique selling proposition. They set you apart from the competition, giving you a recognizable identity as an actor. They build demand for your talent. They are your area of expertise, your place in the market.

Your Castable Types are the roles or characters you not only play well but embody, then relate fully and authentically to the audience or camera. They are the roles which, from the point of view of casting directors, agents and theatrical directors, fit you as an actor because you live the role and energize the material. Your Castable Types are the roles you portray more effectively than other actors in the commercial and theatrical arena, both emotionally and physically.

Your Castable Types will change and develop over time. You will outgrow some and mature into new ones. This will happen naturally, not just because of the number of candles on your birthday cake but because you have aged, ripened and matured. Think again about the actress I described at the beginning of this chapter. Even though she looked seven or eight years younger than most people her age, her personality, body language, and vocal cadence all radiated a take-charge energy. In a 22 year old, that energy would likely read as excitement, self assurance, impatience to get going in life. In my 29 year old client, that energy read as someone who had confidence born of experience, who had excitement for life because she had figured out what she wanted to do and be and the patience to know that, in time, it would all happen. Each actress could be described as young, confident and energetic but they are actually two very different Castable Types. They would deliver strikingly different readings at an audition for the same role. Is one better than the other? Of course not. One would, though, be more appropriate for the part. Knowing what roles you are truly best suited for and then prepping for them, is another benefit of understanding and using your Castable Types. One that agents and managers demand in today's competitive, fast moving casting world.

Your Castable Types will evolve and expand with cultural and social changes. An actor who expertly exudes an introverted braininess would have found his roles limited to bespectacled geeks with pocket protectors years ago. One internet revolution later and that same actor could play the tech genius with the rock star lifestyle, political blogger, social media master or key part of a heroic, save-the-world-from-evil team. Viral video, reality television and 24 hour news channels are driving forces for introducing new types into the public consciousness that writers incorporate into scripts. Staying on top of trends is a smart tactic to spot ways to expand your Castable Types and overall castability.

Your Castable Types are shaped in part by your physical appearance. Societal and cultural influences expand the definitions of beauty, masculinity, fitness and what is "camera ready." In most cases, your appearance should give definition to your Castable Types rather than determine them.

Other facets of appearance which inform your Castable

Types are physical life and voice. These are outward aspects of your energy that are very relatable to the camera or audience. A beautiful full-figured actor with a smoldering voice, who brings sensual intensity to words and movement across the stage or on camera can be far more compelling than a thin model who moves and speaks self-consciously. Bringing your look into harmony with your Castable Types is crucial to developing your talent to a professional level and often easier than you might think.

Your Castable Types are not a form of type casting. They do not pigeonhole you. They do not limit your talent to one physical, vocal or personality trait. Developing and defining what is unique about your talent gives agents and casting directors a clear idea of where to place you in the casting process or on their client roster. You are showing them your possibilities and potential in a way that makes business sense. That means you have a far better chance of getting representation by an agent or manager who knows what roles to submit you for and casting offices calling you in for what you have the strongest chance to book. This is especially important if you are an emerging actor with few credits or reentering the industry after a break. Your marketing materials and audition monologues must support and reinforce your Castable Types.

RECOGNIZING YOUR CASTABLE TYPES

To recognize your Castable Types you need to let go of all past assumptions and preconceived notions about yourself and your work. You need to think like an expert acting coach and use the perspective of a casting director. An expert coach looks at your talent and the way you market it in terms of working at a professional level. A casting director will only see you filtered through the work you perform at an audition and the impression made by your marketing materials. If you rely on the opinions of family, friends and other actors who know you, your moods and habitual behaviors intimately, you will not get accurate feedback. Some of what they know to be you will certainly come through in your acting but a casting director won't *react* to any of it the way family and friends will.

The same holds true for a drama teacher lacking experience at casting calls or go-see's. His or her input will be more informed by the progress and potential of your work in class than where it really is now.

So, if you can't meet with me, you will have to step in to the mindset of a casting professional and play the role of and expert coach to get started. Here's how to do it.

THE CASTABLE TYPE TEST

To evaluate an actor's Castable Types, I first get a handle on how the industry now views him. Headshots, resume credits and a rundown of what he gets called in to read and what he books give me some answers. If the actor has representation and who that representation is, gives me more information.

Next, I want to see if the industry is seeing the talent and uniqueness that is really living inside the actor or if it's hidden away, yet to be discovered. To do that, I have him perform a prepared monologue of his own choosing and then do five or six cold readings I've selected. I use a mix of commercial copy, monologues and scenes from film and television. Most of the material is more expository and behavioral than action-driven. I want to see, hear and feel what the actor can do with the script rather than what the script does for the actor. In initial auditions, you rarely get the most dramatic or action driven material to read for much the same reason. Any first year acting student can cry like a baby and yell up a storm. It takes a great deal more expertise to be alive, in the moment and sustain the emotional throughline when the character is not in the midst of a tantrum or breakdown.

Once I get a feel for the actor's Castable Types, the last one or two cold reading selections will be chosen more specifically to challenge the depth of the qualities that are most striking.

No matter the level of experience, ability to do cold readings or quality of the monologue performance, at least one Castable Type will emerge. Often two or three. Some are very specific and others more general and in need of definition.

The notes I take while the actor works through the material focus on the choices he makes and the manner and degree to which he realizes them fully.

Choices demonstrate talent and technique. An actor's talent is in the depth and breadth of the empathy he has for his character. Technique is the ability to bring that empathy and understanding to life in performance. A prepared monologue should have the clearest, most resonant choices since the actor had time to work on it. That isn't always the case. The cold readings, which most actors struggle with, require quicker, more instinctive choices based on a cursory reading of the script or sides. The unique, physical and emotional qualities the actor repeatedly relates to me and the camera, which bring the roles to life, are the basis of his Castable Types.

❑❑❑❑

You can do this on your own by recording yourself performing the same types of material in the same limited time frame. Reviewing your own acting can be difficult if you get caught up in judgments about your appearance or pick apart every detail of your work. It serves no purpose. Again, the more you can approach this with the mindset of an expert coach and casting professional, the more value it will be to your career.

I know well how much actors love to have the opinions of others to boost their self-esteem or provide that missing pearl of wisdom. But the understanding of what makes your talent unique and how your choices read on camera is insight that will improve your work and confidence in a much greater way than mere compliments or general suggestions. A practical working knowledge of your Castable Types is the key to unlocking the door to acting success.

To stay on track with your self-evaluation, avoid sweeping critiques. You aren't writing a review. Look at how well each of the elements of your acting is realized and then what the strongest, most vibrant ones add up to as potential Castable Types.

EVALUATING YOUR WORK

Read through all the points I use before recording your own work for evaluation. Answer them once based on what you now believe to be true about your work, then a second time, based solely on what you see on playback. Keep your answers brief and incisive, just as a casting director might at an open call.

What is your relatability quotient?

Sit in on any casting session, especially for commercials, and you will hear the phrase, "relate to the camera". It's one of the most common adjustments actors get at auditions. The ability to connect what is going on inside you to the camera is your *relationship* with the camera. The strength and clarity of that connection is the degree to which you are *relating* to the camera. If the actor relies on words to carry the emotional throughline or directed actions to maintain energy, he will not *relate* effectively to the camera. If you never book commercial jobs, this is probably the reason. Embracing your Castable Types will totally resolve this issue.

What inherent or distinguishing personality traits do you bring to the role?

Every role has a breakdown: a description of the inherent or distinguishing personality traits of the character that the actor must bring to life. Some breakdowns are minimal, others as long as an essay. In either case, the breakdown is the foundation of the character—not the limit. Actors who meld their inherent or distinguishing personality traits to those of the character, then allow their personality to develop the part even more, own the role. This is a hallmark of Castable Type acting.

What physical traits do you integrate naturally and effectively into your acting?

As with personality traits, physical traits must be brought fully to life. At most on-camera auditions an actor has to stand on a mark to be recorded. That doesn't mean you're locked into a stance and stare position. Physical life is an expression of the character's energy and helps create the reality of place and circumstance. Integrating your physical traits naturally and effectively with the character's brings nuanced behaviors to your acting. This is a key element of performance level work that you can achieve using the Castable Types technique.

How well do you realize emotional transitions?

As mentioned earlier in the chapter, most audition material is more behavioral than action-driven, but that doesn't mean the story is static. Emotional transitions are the true drivers of a storyline. They exist in every script and piece of commercial copy, no matter how short or nonlinear. Perhaps the most important emotional transition is the one that happens before the lines begin, known as the Prior Moment. If that is missed or only partially realized, the work is flat and disconnected. If you cannot find and support the emotional transitions, especially the Prior Moment, your acting will be technical, flat and lifeless. Your work will be missing all that you could bring to it and you will be short changing your talent.

Are you able to find and stay true to the pace of the material?

Pace is a key element to any performance. If you are using a "beat to beat" approach to the script you will always get the pace and most other crucial elements wrong. When your pace is off, you have nothing to carry you to the next emotional transition. It's like

25

slogging through waist deep snow. You have to take extra time, extra pauses, indicate what is happening inside the character because it didn't happen organically within the action and dialogue. At the same time, you get so driven by the words that the pace is too fast to experience the character's inner life. This cuts off your ability to infuse a role with nuanced behaviors that bring your Castable Types to the work.

Do you have any physical or vocal ticks or mannerisms?
Sometimes mistaken for physical life, emotional transition or authentic behavior, ticks and mannerisms are a product of tension and nerves. They are an indication of how disconnected the actor is to the character due to a lack of relaxation and preparation. They distract from a performance, quickly becoming an annoyance. If you find your work is peppered with repetitive movements, gestures, reactions through your voice or body that are really commentary, you have a blockage that needs to be excised from your work to let your talent and personality shine through.

What style, demeanor and overall image can you convey authentically?
Some people exude authority in the way they walk. They have an edgy, unpredictable quality no matter the situation. Others sound educated and cultured reading the ingredient list off the side of a cereal box. We all project an image. Most actors can project two or three different, distinct images well. Sometimes, the visual image is broken or changes completely once we begin speaking and other times our voice and cadence amplify it.

In evaluating Castable Types, image matters. It's more than just appearance, although this is where height, size, shape and age range are considered. It's the total package and the energy that supports it. The range of images, styles and demeanors you can convey believably give texture and definition to your Castable Types.

There are many factors to consider in evaluating this area. Some fit perfectly with one or two of your Castable Types, others, may not be useful elements for you when compared to other actors. Avoid dated ideas like glossy, over-styled soap opera shots that have little application or meaning in today's industry.

Look instead for demeanor, style and image cues that enhance each of your Castable Types, conveying their energy even when you aren't speaking lines.

Below are specific elements of image and descriptive terms I use often to define it in evaluations:

Demeanor: approachable, nurturing, authoritarian, edgy, dangerous, rough, innocent, sensual, quirky, neurotic, driven, intellectual, sensuous, reserved, crotchety, cool, slick.

Movement: fluid, awkward, plodding, smooth, slow, quick, big, careful, considered, explosive, comedic, mechanical, balletic

Style: polished, educated, bohemian, indie, urban, suburban, laid back, hip, intense, sexy, powerful, gentle, gracious, gruff, dated, disheveled, sporty, matronly, fresh, cultured.

With the next three sections, consider each of points listed and note the answers.

Voice: vocal quality, cadence, diction, accents, speech impediments, languages spoken

Physical Appearance: age range, size, shape, healthy, showing some wear and tear, nationalities (that the actor could reasonably be cast as), character-type features (facial tattoos, green hair, pronounced scars, obvious dental issues that cannot or will not be addressed, etc)

Pluses: are there any special or added factors that should be considered? This usually leads to an actor being able to play a very specific character with a high degree of believability. The traits of that character wouldn't be apparent unless the actor is reading for that part (I see this a lot with actors who have absorbed a person in their life so thoroughly that they don't imitate the person—they inhabit him (Bosses and in-laws are a common example). It could also be specialized knowledge of a subject. If you can toss the lingo or tools connected with that subject around with ease in a cold reading or improvisation audition, factor this into your Castable Type consideration

❏❐❏❐

Compare your before and after notes. It's very common to realize that aspects of your acting you thought were strong and defining are not, while others you never considered have a much stronger impact. You may also be seeing for the first time that you've been ignoring crucial elements of Performance Level work that casting directors need to see in auditions and call backs to seriously consider you for a role. If that's the case, don't have a meltdown or beat yourself up. You have highly beneficial information that can now be used to improve your acting skills and better your auditions and performances. The process of understanding what elements of your essential spirit bring life to a role and how you can make that a recognizable identity, strengthening your ability to succeed in the casting process and book work, is the creation of your Castable Types. It's worth a little wince and groan if it leads to ownership of your acting career.

WHAT ARE MY CASTABLE TYPES?

The answer is to consider your evaluation notes and then answer these questions:

—What roles, currently seen in the genres I am interested in working (i.e., primetime television, indie film, musical theatre, etc.), could I play better than at least 90% of the competition?

—What Castable Types now established in the industry do I now fully or partially embody?

—What new Castable Type could I introduce to industry or a specific genre?

The answers to these three questions, based on the work you evaluated—not on what you would like your work to be, is what determines your Castable Types today.

If you're looking at your notes and still feel indecisive, this real life example of my work with a client should give you guidance. You'll notice I give each of her Castable Types a name and a breakdown. This helps bring the type to life. It encourages the actor to spot traits shared with roles encountered at auditions as well as key differences. It also helps in the process of bringing them to marketing materials, like headshots, in a very vibrant way. More on that, in later chapters.

A CASE STUDY

Below are my evaluation notes for a talented actress named Skyler. She did a series of cold readings and a prepared monologue so we could determine her Castable Types and areas of technique that require coaching. I make one set of notes for all the pieces performed, separating the traits and qualities with a/mark.

Castable Type Evaluation: Skyler
Relatability: connects but could be stronger/present but in a detached way

29

Personality Traits: ambitious, driven, demands a great deal of herself and expects the same from others/wants to please, can't always live up to her own tough standards, afraid to disappoint/eager to learn and experience as much as she can as quickly as possible/college, experimental, risk-taking, partier

Physical Traits: purposeful, bold/feeling of powerful inner life being contained/sexy, knows how to attract attention without being obvious

Emotional Transitions: weak prior moments/connects well once into the text but misses many transitions/takes adjustments well; can definitely learn technique to improve this

Pace: rushes/hits first words of sentences and phrases

Ticks: clips some of her words and cadence/lots of big arm gestures

Demeanor/Style: privileged, educated, mature/college, experimental, risk-taking/sexy, alluring in a reserved way

Movement: purposeful, tight/comedic, theatrical, playful/statuesque

Style: polished /college casual/clean and classic

Physical Appearance: 5.8+, long limbs, attractive, healthy, trim, plays early 20's, hair is too long and overpowers her face

Voice: warm with casual dialogue/naturally authoritative rest of the time/cannot do any accents well

Pluses: insider knowledge of politics/can play drunk & hung over well/strong facility with classical dialogue

Goals: She wants to pursue work in the commercial and print markets, film and classical theatre.

❑❐❑❐

From the evaluation and a discussion of her career goals, we defined three Castable Types as follows:

1. The Type A Grad Student/Emerging Professional:
   Driven, goal-oriented, highly intelligent, with the need or the bad habit of flaunting it to show she

belongs with the power crowd or to feel superior or put someone in his place. When this person is in her zone, she is in charge, on top of it and highly productive. When she lets her guard down, disappoints or experiences failure, she crashes.

Representative Roles: a political staffer/intern, med or law school student, activist, junior agent, television producer

2. The Icy Cool Beauty:

Confident in her physical beauty to the point that she views it as an asset in the capitalist sense. She would prefer that a man invest in her pet project or her pay her rent than fall in love with her. She is comfortable having others wait on her. She enjoys the finer things in an understated way and wants little to do with people her own age. She has plans. Big plans. Rules can be bent in her pursuit of them.

Representative Roles: the competition (to the lovable female lead), the trust-fund society daughter, the untouchable heartbreaker

3. The Roommate/College Best Friend:

The best friend who is liked by all, grounded, normal, drama-free. The one who doesn't embarrass herself at the party or puke in the bar bathroom. The girl the guys seek out for advice. The quirky lead's best friend. The only girl on the team who plays well. One of the guys.

Representative Roles: the roommate, the resident advisor, the college athlete

At first glance—and let's face it, most actors only get a first glance be it in person or with their headshot—an agent or casting director would look at Skyler and think attractive, young, friendly and declare her a romantic comedy type. That generalization would be off base and lead to much wasted creative, emotional and financial capital for Skyler. In auditions for a typical rom-com leading lady, she would never fit the role better than other actors at the reading. She would never embody the lighthearted, dreamy, often goofy nature the story usually demands of that character. She is well suited for that kind of vehicle, but in a very different role.

A better, smarter move for Skyler's acting career is to identify and build on the traits that she has naturally and use them to differentiate her from the competition, making her more castable. She and I accomplished this using the Castable Type Technique and the Complete Thought Approach which addresses pace, connection and relatability by bringing more of her unique qualities to her acting and marketing materials.

Through a Castable Type approach to her acting and marketing, Skyler is now presenting her talent in its most viable light. In today's industry, with its fast casting demands, that is a requirement for career success. Agents and managers don't have time to spend getting to know you and your talent. They don't have time to discover the unique selling proposition in your work. It's up to you to know it, develop it, use it in auditions and your marketing tools and make it crystal clear to your representation. Then your agent or manager can do a better job of selling you to casting directors. You and your team have the right tools to get the job done.

DISCOVERING THE MOST VIABLE MARKETS FOR YOUR CASTABLE TYPES

When you have a solid, working understanding of your Castable Types you will find it much easier to identify the strongest opportunities to book work. You will begin to notice the films, television shows, commercials, print ads and theatrical productions that use the characters you can bring to life better than the competition. Invest time and energy in researching the writers and creative teams behind these vehicles. Follow their work, read their scripts, look for interviews with them on-line. Get to know where they have shown their films or had their plays produced and where they will be next. Find out what directors they partner with or hope to work with in the future. Learn all you can about what influences their work. In the case of commercials, hit the internet to discover quickly the advertising agency and creative team behind the campaigns you should be booking. Most advertising pros have a reel on-line and plenty of blurbs and quotes in the trades, all of which you should be studying.

This research gives you a chance to get ahead of the competition. If you know where your Castable Types are used, have insight into the writers who create the dialogue, the directors who shape the story and have a say in final casting and where or when the next opportunity to connect will be, you have an edge. You can then target the casting offices that will be doing the auditions and agents and managers who have strong relationships with those offices. If you already have an agent or a manager, you can let them know these are the projects and roles you believe you have the strongest chance to book. Ask them to get you an audition slot when casting starts so you can prove it.

Understanding and leveraging the power of your Castable Types holistically, so they inform and benefit your acting career in every possible way, will open doors to opportunities of real value. You will put yourself in the right place, at the right time, in your own, special light. Embracing a new approach can feel like a struggle at first. The real struggle is pursuing your passion and staying excited when every opportunity feels like a lost cause. If you are stuck in outdated thinking, yesterday's rules and a passive mentality, you will struggle indefinitely. Hard work, dedication and a love of the art of acting will get you much further if you're playing your hot hand. That's your Castable Types. The time and effort you put into developing and using them through this technique is an investment in your career that you can leverage within the industry for greater access and opportunity. The next step in that process is to develop your Castable Types and bring them to your work.

CHAPTER 2

THE CASTABLE TYPE MONOLOGUE

The key to fully developing and using your Castable Types is through extensive, in-depth monologue work. This work will then be applied in auditions, cold readings, performances and on-camera situations, including headshot shoots. The key tool in this process is creating a library of monologues, brought to performance level, exemplifying your Castable Types and the variations within.

WHY MONOLOGUES?

When a monologue is performed successfully, an actor is fully immersed in the life of the character, holding a connection with the audience that transcends words. Mastery of monologues is mastery of the craft of acting.

Being in the audience of a stellar, one person show is a mesmerizing experience. It's like auditing an acting master class. The physical presence, sensorial involvement and emotional clarity the performer on stage has with his character(s) is total. For the majority of solo shows, the set is minimal and props limited. yet, there is far more nuanced behavior and energy by that one person on stage who is carrying the entire production alone. The throughline, subtext and stakes are all the actor has to depend on to draw in and hold the audience. It is as reductive in concept as it is limitless in effect, a truly magical experience when accomplished well.

I've been lucky enough to see many of the best one person shows of the last thirty years—Ben Kingsley in *Edmund*

Kean, Alec McCowen in *Kipling*, Lily Tomlin in *The Search for Signs of Intelligent Life in the Universe,* Pauline Collins in *Shirley Valentine,* a breathtaking Antony Sher in *Primo* and my personal favorite, Mike Daisey in *How Theatre Failed America* and *If You See Something Say Something.* I've also sat through torturous shows starring A-list actors, whose award winning work was painfully absent as they struggled to inhabit a role and engage the audience.

It is a measure of talent and technique to perform a monologue well, whether it is on stage, on film or television. You may be able to bounce along believably through a passage of dialogue with the energy of another actor to keep you in the moment but there is a great deal more required to creating and performing a role of greater substance and impact, be it comedic, dramatic or somewhere in between. The ability to do that is the difference between an actor who books the featured and starring roles and the one who never does better than under-fives. It is one reason why agents and managers ask to see monologues. That one-minute performance in the agency office speaks volumes about your readiness to work professionally and what resources an agent or manager should invest in your career.

YOUR CASTABLE TYPE LIBRARY

The work required to bring a monologue to life should be thought of as the research and development of your Castable Types. By mastering solo material that exemplifies your Castable Types, you will be creating a library of unique traits, energies and behaviors in specific emotional and physical situations. These will become the reference points for making informed choices when approaching new material. The life contained within each monologue will be transferrable to roles you read for in auditions. It will also provide you with a solid, flexible base for building characters you will play in the future. We'll cover how to do that in depth in Chapters 4 and 5. First, the material needs to be selected.

Necessary elements of the best Castable Type monologues

Choosing monologues for your library should be fun; an expression of your creativity. You aren't looking for a single, perfect monologue to marry to a Castable Type. You are looking for many monologues to personify each Castable Type in a variety of tones and styles. This benefits you in two important ways. First, by allowing characteristics of a particular type to be explored in more depth and, second, in a range of genre styles. The more material you can master, the more options you will have at your disposal.

Consider one of the Castable Types discussed in the previous chapter, the Icy, Cool, Beauty. There are many contemporary monologues an actress could choose to bring specific elements of this character to life in both a comedic and dramatic way. Also to be considered are the markets in which the actress would like to work. In this instance, in film, commercials and classical theatre. She could certainly use one of Olivia's monologues from Shakespeare's Twelfth Night to embody confidence born of physical beauty, ease in the world of privilege, plotting and planning to obtain a (romantic) goal and a cool, cultured demeanor. This would give her one option for classical auditions. She should have several more in this one area to emphasis other aspects of this type. Just because this choice is classical, does not preclude its use in other, contemporary situations. If the core of the character developed from the material or even one or two key traits, will bring commercial copy to life, it would be foolish to not use it.

There are certain, necessary qualities you should look for when choosing a Castable Type monologue. These will ensure your choice of script is solid enough to support the research and development you want to accomplish through it.

Fresh material

Dated, hackneyed monologues will never serve you well. The same holds true for material that is closely identified with a particular actor. This is a crucial point for younger actors and anyone new to the business to keep in mind. What may be fresh to you might be all too familiar to an industry pro with a few more years in the business. That is the person who will be looking at and listening to your work. If an agent has seen the material performed for years, you are setting yourself up for comparison with all the actors who have gone before.

Monologues can resemble fashion trends in that certain pieces are all the rage for a season or two. The work from which it is taken may have been a breakthrough vehicle for the writer or the actor who originated the role may have garnered critical attention. If you are inexorably drawn to that monologue, you must make it your own but stay true to its context if the original production is still in the mind of the industry. This was something I was able to do for myself many years ago with a wonderful monologue from a Craig Lucas play. It was the monologue of the moment for actresses in my age range. Everyone was using it at auditions. I knew I could do a better job with it than my competition. The material would benefit from a more nuanced emotional connection and physical reality to have effect without hysterics. The script required the character expose her rawest nerve without falling apart. Raw nerves are a strong Castable Type quality in my work! I had developed that into an element I could relate to fully, with energy, on a consistent basis. When the opportunity to audition, first for a top agent and later for an A list film director, came my way, I made the decision to do this monologue. I knew I would be compared to others who were doing the same material. I would have to nail it from the first to last moment if my talent was to stand out. Thankfully, I did just that. After my audition for the agent, she took a moment and then said she had heard the monologue many times in the past six months but never heard it "quite like that." Yes, it felt like an eternity while I waited for her to finish the sentence. She continued by saying that she "never realized what the monologue could really be" until she heard me do it and that she was "blown away." The director, who did not hire me to be in the film I auditioned for, instead called me a year later with an offer for another project, said she had "never forgotten my work." A very calculated risk paid off big time for me in those two situations.

If you feel as connected to a monologue as I did to that one and are equally confident in your ability to do better than all the others who may also be using it, go for it. If not, look for something fresh that experienced ears will want to hear.

Exposure over exposition

In the previous chapter, I mentioned that material used at auditions tends to be expository rather than climactic. casting directors want to see an actor bring the role to life rather than cold read the character's biggest moment or try to pantomime through an action sequence. When looking for Castable Types monologues, you want exposure rather than exposition for a very similar reason. Exposure will allow you to bring the role to life rather than tell the story of the script. It lets you engage in behavior and have full involvement right from the start. You do not want to preface or explain what your character is experiencing, you simply want to live it.

The structure of the monologue does not need a beginning, middle and end defined by words alone. The emotional transition of the character is what drives the action from start to finish.

Just as a film may begin with a fade-in to a scene in progress, a good monologue will open at full strength. If the piece has to build a head of steam or get to a punch line to be interesting, an actor will be tied up in exposition and line delivery. Choose material that engages the audience in the life of your character right from the start.

Appearance appropriate

It may seem obvious to write that the role in the monologue should be appearance-appropriate but in my experience coaching, it often is not. Regardless of the personal connection an actor may feel for the character, it will not serve the purpose intended if physical incongruity is always in the mind of the audience. Especially if that audience is an agent or casting director.

There is material that can be tweaked or lightly edited to adjust for gender, size or age without subverting the piece. There is a great deal more material that suffers in that process.

One of the biggest benefits of the Castable Types approach is taking ownership of a role. That happens when you fuse your unique qualities into those of the character. If you are able to do it in every way except appearance, that schism becomes a distraction which undermines your work. Imagine a classic role like Willy Loman from *Death of a Salesman* played by a fit, handsome actor in his 40's. It doesn't work for the audience and won't benefit the performer.

Developing these monologues requires the integration of your physical appearance into the material through your Castable Types. One informs the other. As you make your monologue selections, consider the character's appearance. What image comes to mind? How easily and authentically do you project that image? If simple adjustments make your appearance and the material appropriate for each other, great. If not, move on to other choices.

OWN A WRITER

One of the goals of this approach is to "own" a role. When you do find and master a monologue that blows your competition out of the water, take a careful look at other work by the same writer. If there are additional vehicles with characters perfectly suited to your talent, why not become the go-to actor for that writer's work? Don't just own the role, own the writer.

You can avoid repetition by tackling more obscure or earlier material. Look for scripts your chosen writer did in collaboration with someone else or for a different market. Many playwrights also write for film and television; screenwriters will take on the stage. A little research may uncover rarely performed short form work for festivals. The complete script may be uneven but there could be a hidden gem of a monologue waiting to be discovered.

When looking for Castable Type monologues, invest the time and effort needed to get material that gives your talent a place to soar. Try on monologues the way you try on clothing: keep going until the fit is just right. Once you have the right material, it's time to get to get busy bringing it to life. Which means it's also time to think long and hard about the technique you've been using in your acting work. You can't make the most of your new career insights if you don't have a reliable, proven, professional approach to acting that takes your work to its very best. To get big results with your Castable Types, you need a complimentary acting technique that continues the holistic makeover of your career.

CHAPTER 3

THE CASTABLE TYPES APPROACH TO ACTING

OPPORTUNITY VS. PANIC

When handed a script, the average actor will plow through it eagerly, making mental notes of the number of lines he has, how likable his character is and how his role compares to others in the project. Thoughts of using an exercise or two learned in acting class will cross the actor's mind. Perhaps sense memory, substitution, an animal or repetition exercise will be considered, then quickly dropped, in favor of getting down to business and memorizing those lines. An actor can't be faulted if his lines are drilled into his brain and firmly locked in his voice and body, can he? He may not be able to make adjustments or bring much life to the character when he isn't saying lines, but he won't be at risk of making artistic mistakes, getting criticized for his work and feeling like a fool. Besides, someone will tell him what to do and how to do it. He just has to show up and say the lines.

Right?

Not by a long shot.

There is so much that is wrong with this all too common scenario but I can sum it up for you in two words: *Panic Acting*.

WHY YOU SUCK

Panic Acting is when an actor shuts down creativity and flow in an attempt to mistake-proof his work by making no choices at all, focusing instead on the delivery of memorized lines and the indication of superficial emotion and behavior.

This results in recitation rather than performance, cutting off creativity, nuance, connection and the ability to respond to adjustments and directorial demands.

Realizing he is blowing it big time, the actor will attempt to salvage his reading by acting out all the punctuation in the script to prove he is intelligent and has some understanding of the work.

The final outcome is always an uninspiring, wooden, totally forgettable, reading by the actor. At auditions, this frustrates the casting associates by wasting time and energy, making them wonder why the actor is even in the business of acting when he just chose not to act. On the set, it exasperates the director beyond belief. He needs the actor to do the job of acting so he can do his job as director.

All of which results in the actor getting a reputation for sucking.

The root of bad acting

So why, when jobs are few and far between and opportunities to use talent and creativity are so precious, do so many actors make the totally self-defeating choice of Panic Acting?

There are three reasons:

1. Not understanding why you were cast in a role over other actors
2. Fear
3. Lack of a straightforward, reliable, proven technique for approaching a role that is accessible to the actor in auditions and performances.

When you don't understand why you were cast in a role over other actors or why you even booked the job at all, your actor's mind goes to dark, scary places. You doubt that your talent got you the job. You doubt your look is right for the part. You doubt that the casting person was paying attention and maybe hired you by mistake; or worse, as an act of desperation. Maybe no one else wanted the role. Maybe it is such a lousy, unimportant part that no other actor would take it. So it was offered to you. The actor with the giant "L" for Loser on his forehead.

In the previous chapter we explored how defining and developing your Castable Types is the key to unlocking success as a professional actor. Strengthening and then using the unique and essential qualities that make up your Castable Types in performance level work brings specificity, energy, relatability and nuance to every role. That is what casting directors look for in actors. That is what gets you to the final callback. That is what persuades a director to take a risk on a fresh face or an actor who differs from the breakdown and give him or her a chance.

If you are fully utilizing the power of your Castable Types in every aspect of your acting career, from marketing materials to performance, you will get the benefit of feeling secure in the fact that it is *you* and your unique qualities that got you the part and is what you are expected to bring to the role. That is the person who should be making the choices that drives the work that is expected at the audition and on the set.

Having your Castable Types as a guidepost is a big benefit to an actor. Our job is to expose a character emotionally in front of an audience or camera while creating a sense of authenticity and connection through behavior, action and reaction. It's not something that can be accomplished when you question why you booked the job and your ability to do it well.

That feeling of doubt leads to reason #2, fear.

Once fear creeps into your mind, it starts chipping away at the choices you do make when creating a role. It makes you second guess your most basic decisions, even your understanding of the script, sending your choices and work off in the wrong direction. It destroys your relaxation which shuts down your instrument and your connection to the character. When these things happen you are no longer functioning as an actor. Your unique Castable Type disappears. The physical energy, emotional life and nuanced behaviors you should bring to the role are unable to flow through you to the camera or audience. The work is no longer relatable as it's now trapped in your head and blocked by tension in your body. You essentially vanish from the role.

Fear and doubt makes the idea of focusing on line memorization so much more appealing and safe. It absolves the actor of making real choices and personally connecting to the work. It gives the actor cover by demonstrating that time and effort was put into the role even though it was only rote work. The actor is, for all practical purposes, palming off the work of creating and bringing a role to life on the director or coasting on dialogue with other characters.

MISSING THE RIGHT TOOLS

Panic Acting wouldn't happen if the actor had a solution to reason #3 and possessed a straight-forward, reliable, proven technique for approaching a role through his Castable Types that is easily accessible in auditions and performances. Even well-trained actors rarely have this in their toolkits. Such a technique is a tool of creative independence for a performing artist. That is not something college drama programs, conservatories and career studios provide. It's not what they do. It's not in their business plan. It doesn't benefit their bottom line. It doesn't add to their mystique or keep them in business.

There are few training programs that teach truly effective audition and performance skills which meet the audition and performance demands of the industry today.

University and conservatory programs focus on exploration of the art of acting or are taught as auteur programs focusing on a heritage technique. Their curricula are designed to create educated artists, not necessarily working artists. Long hours in the classroom conquering scene work of dramatic merit but often skewed for age and type, are tough to translate into a professional application. Teaching up-to-date audition and working skills is an afterthought if it's even a thought at all. Most of the instructors are comfortably immersed in this *art for art's sake* setting and lose touch with the world of professional auditions, marketing one's talent and the requirements of booking work as it's done today. If a program even allows faculty to incorporate the teaching of this additional material, few would be able to offer anything of relevance.

Career studios claim to offer more practical training and an understanding of the audition and work process but they aren't set up to teach these skills either. It's not in their financial interest to screen out clients with no acting skills or actors with no concept of the work required to master those skills and effort it takes to book professional jobs. It's not profitable to develop content-rich, extended courses for that drop-in clientele seeking a shortcut to success. Courses taught by working actors and directors experienced teaching actual acting technique don't attract new clients the way one led by a casting director does, even though all a casting director will do is give you cold readings and then critique your pseudo-audition.

It's cheaper and easier for career studios to sell industry access to actors with more hope than sense and call it a workshop. Nor is it their business model to have clients get to a point where they've mastered the skills to work and stop buying that access. There's more profit in keeping things short, simple and superficial.

❑❑❑❑

I'm a big believer in serious, continuing and contextual training. If you check out my c.v., you'll see I've studied and trained long and hard, with some of the most gifted figures in the industry, past and present, in some of the most rigorous and exclusive degree programs in the English-speaking world. That training and my commitment to it shaped me into the artist I am today. For that, I am profoundly grateful to every one of my brilliant teachers and mentors.

Yet, once out in the professional arena I quickly realized that, despite my elite training and perceived artistic genius, I was still missing the right tools to book paying jobs consistently and an understanding of how to leverage my talent to agents, casting directors and the industry.

So, like you, I spent plenty of my hard earned money at career studios hoping to fill in the gaps of my university and conservatory training. Probably like you, I was sorely disappointed.

Career studios aren't bad places. There is a need for the industry exposure they sell as long as the actors are ready for it and the industry guests are actively seeking fresh talent. They just don't provide what most actors who use them truly need, a technique to free them of bad habits, synergize the grab bag of acting skills acquired over years of disparate training, that takes their unique energy and understanding of the industry to a professional level, maximizing castability.

GETTING AND ACCEPTING WHAT YOU NEED

The goal of Part II of this book is for you to use the power of your Castable Types holistically in every facet of your acting career.

First, by understanding that the industry will view you by the qualities and energy you radiate most, which determines your Castable Types. That gets your foot in the agents and casting director's door.

Next, by strengthening, enhancing and bringing your Castable Types to life through monologue work. This allows you to do the deep exploration of and make personal connections to representative roles you will infuse with your unique energy and make your own.

Once you've mastered a library of Castable Type monologues you can apply that research and development in auditions and on the set to make quick, clear, inspired choices at a professional performance level.

Now, to do it all, you're going to need that reliable, proven, easily accessible technique for approaching a role and integrating your Castable Types into the work. You need what you've been missing, even though you may have years of training under your belt.

You will need to make room for a fresh approach to let go of panic behaviors and bad habits. Once the slate is clean, you will be able to embrace a simpler, deeper way of working that brings more of you to the part. It can't happen any other way. Nor is it as easy to do as it sounds.

PANIC VS. OPPORTUNITY

You're probably thinking to yourself, why wouldn't I embrace what I need? In truth, most actors don't, and by choice.

When you've been working hard learning the craft of acting and struggling with its many elements, but still come up short booking jobs, it's disillusioning, especially if you have to defend your career choice or justify the high cost of training to family and friends. That makes many actors cling defensively to the grab bag of techniques and bad habits repeated failure instills in an attempt to save face and keep the dream alive.

If you don't let go of what doesn't get results, no matter how habitual, entrenched or intellectually appealing the technique, you won't attain your dream. It's okay to say aloud the training you paid to learn, struggled to understand and probably had a few classroom breakdowns over, if not a public beat down by the instructor, isn't giving you everything you need. It was likely developed decades ago for a different generation of actors and a different aesthetic of writing, directing and production styles.

All was not wasted. The craft of acting is evolutionary. We all benefit from the contributions of the great teachers. Any individual exercise that is reliably effective for you in specific situations, can and should remain. The core of naturalistic acting, as Stanislavsky realized, is rooted in relaxation of the instrument. The connections made through Strasberg's sense memory work are key elements of many great performances because the power of personal truth is timeless. Many of the introductory exercises of the Meisner school teach the concept of being in the moment quickly and painlessly.

These individual elements are now so basic that, once understood and practiced, should be second nature to a professional. They just aren't enough on their own to support a performance, as any working actor can attest. It's understanding when and how to use all the other puzzle pieces that have been thrown at you that causes the mess.

What worked in drama school or studio training but doesn't in professional situations is baggage you cannot af-

49

ford to carry any longer. Why would you want to anyway? Because you have the notion drummed into your head that there is a right way and a wrong way to act? Because other actors claim to use a particular technique so you should, too? Because it's not the technique that's failing you, it's your talent?

⌑⌐⌑⌐

After years and years spent in classes, rehearsals and shoots, as actor, coach and director, I kept seeing the same deficiencies in the work of my colleagues and clients. I was giving the same notes a thousand times to 99% of the actors with whom I worked. Repeatedly, I would meet with looks of bewilderment and confusion as these actors tried to make the necessary adjustments to their work. No one could bring it to a performance level and make it worth watching once, let alone for five or ten takes or the run of a show. When I asked people to describe how the role was approached, I would hear the most esoteric, nonsensical, unusable, circuitous explanations from the actors you could possibly imagine. I rarely heard anyone speak of the focus on the elements that needed to be realized or an awareness of how to accomplish that.

When I found myself on the casting side of the audition room table, it confirmed that what I had been encountering was a small but statistically accurate sample of a much bigger issue with the quality of training and performance. Auditioning 50 actors for a featured role in a union production, the majority of whom had representation, I would be lucky if two showed me work that was at least memorable. The vast majority of actors were not so much talentless as boring, ordinary, disconnected, physically dead and focused on delivering quickly memorized lines. Every casting session I've ever been a part of was filled with Panic Acting that never rose above tediousness and mediocrity.

Uncertainty and confusion in approaching a role is something every actor deals with at some point in their career. Those who succeed find an approach that works. They use it fearlessly, making the conscious choice to let go of all that doesn't.

Let's move your acting career forward by replacing one of the biggest road blocks to success with something that truly works. Think of this as a fresh approach that will make your Castable Types the heart of your work. Call it an updating, expansion or streamlining of your craft, one that will make your Castable Types the heart of your work. Commit to the release of what works against your talent like memorization, indication, orchestration, and over-thinking. Allow your talent to shine through more and the seams to show less. Embrace the new by clearing out the garbage.

CHAPTER 4

THE COMPLETE THOUGHT TECHNIQUE

FINALLY! A RELIABLE, PROVEN TECHNIQUE

The Castable Types Approach to acting is accomplished through the Complete Thought Technique. This is a practical technique, designed solely for actors, to deconstruct the script from your character's point of view and find the sub-textual gems that make a character resonate with authenticity.

Its six, straight forward steps will give you contextual honesty, let you make inspired creative choices, connect you to the emotional transitions in the script, bring nuanced behavior to your physical life, find perfect pacing and allow depth and energy to infuse your performance.

The first three steps help you analyze a role fully and accurately. The next three steps are the practical, technical applications you will use to bring the role to life through your Castable Types.

The steps are
1. Clean Readings
2. Written Character Profile
3. Prior Moments
4. Complete Thoughts
5. Layering
6. Performance Level

When applied in this order, in the way described, you will see a significant improvement in the quality of your acting plus the added bonus of knowing your lines faster and more accurately, with little or no memorization.

The simplicity of the approach and the performance level work that results is deceptive. Some of the steps may, at first glance, seem familiar. You may have tried elements of any one of them already, though, not with the sustained focus, clarity and concentration required to bring your Castable Types to life through the script at hand. The Complete Thought Approach is unique in this respect. As you gain mastery of each step, you will feel a tremendous difference in your work. A combination of ease, connection and energy that resonates and fills the space in which you are working. Most actors find it hard to define the feeling but are deeply aware of the powerful results. When I work with my private coaching clients, I see the change in their work and in their faces. I call it the Helen Keller moment. You may know the story of this amazing woman from the play or movie, *The Miracle Worker*. As the blind and deaf Helen finally is able to understand that the liquid running over her hand and the letters signed into her open palm both mean water, a connection is made that opens up a world of communication that serves her forever after. Simple, yet incredibly profound. When an actor finds a reliable, understandable technique that unlocks the ability to communicate, to work at a truly advanced level, a world of possibilities opens up. It's why I love this technique, believe in it fully and have so many clients who have turned their careers around by using it.

Let's go through the steps together and in depth.

STEP 1: CLEAN READINGS

It sounds easy, but most actors must learn to read a script with no judgments of their character or concern for the requirements of their role in order to fully comprehend the character as well as the story as a whole.

Think of the last time you read a script in which you had a role. Did you analyze every page in terms of how it affected your part as you read? Did you look at the whole or just stare at your lines? When you began rehearsals or shooting, were you surprised by how little you knew about the other characters? How much of the subtext you missed? How you misinterpreted a few lines?

Now, think about the last script you read for fun, a vehicle that had no part you could possibly play. Did you have a clear understanding of the story? Did the characters stay with you longer? Did you just enjoy it more?

It's through an uninterrupted, start-to-finish, Clean Reading that you get the same understanding of the story as the audience. You grasp not only the whole, you feel its impact. You understand how specific moments, actions or words impel the emotional transitions of the characters. In turn, those transitions drive the events that create the storyline and the individual story arc of each character. When you get that, you get context. Contextual understanding allows you to make informed, accurate choices and maintain your emotional throughline.

That means no stopping and starting to underline, highlight or even make notes. No flipping around to read your character's monologues or major scenes first. No focusing on an action you have to perform in a scene or worry about how to deliver a particular line. No comparing your role to others. No judgments of your character in any way, shape or form. Doing any of these takes you out of the emotional throughline, which diminishes the impact of the story and your contextual understanding of it. It turns your first reading of a script into a rehearsal in your head. You start orchestrating your performance, planning how you will deliver your lines and anticipating ones said by other characters to fit your presuppositions. The emotional proportions of your character become skewed. You *over think* the part, making it impossible to play well.

So, your first step using the Complete Thought Approach is a Clean Reading of the script, uninterrupted from start to finish, without assignment of expression or intention to any part of the dialogue so that every word of the script is heard, every emotional transition experienced, every action realized.

Once you've finished a Clean Reading, sit for a few moments without distraction or reviewing the script. Don't check your messages. Don't hit the fridge. Breathe. Relax. Savor the story the way a gourmand does taste sensation. *The feelings that you now have as a result of this Clean Reading are conveying contextually honest information to you about your character.* This information becomes the guideposts that keep all the rest of your creative choices on track. You don't want to second guess your reactions or contort what you're feeling: the simplicity and clarity of your reactions are key to bringing your unique Castable Type energy to the role. So, without delay, proceed to step two, creating a written character profile.

STEP 2: WRITTEN CHARACTER PROFILE

A combination of script research and personal imagination lays the groundwork for fully developing a character. There are crucial questions every actor must answer and revisit to understand a role and fulfill the needs of the script. Actors often believe they can keep all the vital elements of a character in their head but then lose most of this material in the rush to get off book. A written Character Profile is a requirement if you hope to create a role through your Castable Types and infuse it with your unique energy. The intent is not to juggle copious amounts of notes between your i-pad and your brain but to clarify information gleaned from the script (through your Clean Reading) then make active, insightful choices you can revisit as needed.

Whether you use a tablet of paper or a tablet computer is your personal choice. The content of the profile in an easy to read format so you can refer to it is what matters. A downloadable worksheet is available on my website, www.independentactor.com. Here, I'm going to take you through the content of an effective written profile.

Begin with the feelings that you have as a result of your Clean Reading of the script. Remember, those emotions and reactions are conveying contextually honest information to you about your character the way the writer intended it to reach an audience. Bullet point style phrases are best as you can write or type them quickly and won't get caught up in sentence structure, grammar or syntax. Don't approach this as though it is work to be handed in to the teacher. You aren't trying to impress someone. It's for you. Note your individual impressions in your voice, using your words. Focus on your reaction to the emotional energy of the characters or plot points or the story as a whole. Don't get caught up in statistical facts that don't inform your work. The most basic plot points should have stayed in your brain from the reading. If you are losing them, go back to the first step and do another Clean Reading.

Let's say the script you've just read is about a man named John, on the verge of his 40th birthday, who learns ex-wife, whom he still loves, is about to remarry. Rather than making bullet points that say:

- John is 39 years, 11 months and 28 days old
- He is divorced but still loves his ex-wife
- He still calls her his wife
- He is upset on the inside but seems calm on the outside
- The action takes place en route to the church where the wedding is to be held

Record the emotional energy and your reaction to it instead:
- John is watching the final 48 hours of "the best decade of his life" slip away
- He feels like a man on death row; his ex-wife's wedding in two days is his "execution"
- Everything he sees and does reminds him of her and its making him crazy
- He's unaware of how obsessed he's become and what he is really doing/saying
- John is trying frantically to get to the church before the wedding begins

When you look over your bullet points, key qualities of the character should start to emerge over and over again. With our example role, you see a thread of frustration and desperation. This is the start of the emotional throughline. It is the emotional core of the character. This is what many directors and coaches call the *bottom* of your character. To build a role you must *bottom into your character.* Everything the character sees, hears and does is filtered through this core. If you aren't cognizant of the emotional throughline, the rest of your profile is useless busywork. For instance, if one simply notes where the action of this script is set, let's say a church, what use is that from an acting point of view? None, really. The setting has to be experienced through the filter that is the character's emotional core. In this case, the setting of the church has at least one specific meaning to John that has nothing to do with religion. It could be the place where he believes he can win back his ex-wife, cause a scene and ruin her wedding or where he will finally accept that she is gone and come to terms with his feelings. Each possibility could be salvation or damnation for the character. It is certainly much more than a building or the predictable idea of a house of worship.

The major difference between a written profile using the Complete Thought Technique and what actors are usually advised to do as research is that we are focusing *our* work, what we need to do to bring the character to life. A mere statement of facts already obvious in the script or a journal entry written as the character is busy work. The breakdown or the script will give you the basic who, what, where and when. The writer has already done that job. There is no point in doing it again. Exercises like journal entries can be highly imaginative and potentially lead to a discovery of use. In my coaching experience, I've found most actors either hate doing them and simply rewrite the plot or get totally off track by penning pages and pages of creative writing that has no application to the role—wasted time and energy in both cases.

Professional actors should be able to analyze a script so that the motivation of their character is instantly understandable on an emotional and physical level with contextual accuracy. This is what steps one and two are accomplishing. Your Clean Reading gave you a clear understanding of the whole. If you begin a Written Profile with that information fresh in your mind, it should not get twisted around or misinterpreted. Your initial bullet points are the guideposts to keep you on track. As the Written Profile takes shape, the emotional throughline will emerge in a way that allows you to bottom into the character. Once you have that core understanding, you can now connect your Castable Type energy to the role and infuse your unique traits with the part.

For your Written Profile so far, you should have two sections completed. The first consists of bullet points of your reaction to the entire script (be it monologue, scene or complete script) and of the character you are playing. The next section consists of the emotional throughline as it relates to your character. If you are working on a monologue, the throughline will be relatively brief. If you are tackling a multi-scene role, it is often best to write the throughline for a character as it relates to the entire script and then in segments as they relate to each scene. If you do that, be careful to not lose sight of the full throughline as you segment it. Keep it simple and clean to stay on point. Remember this is the "bottom" of the character. Keep to the core. Going back to our example role of John, his throughline could be:

Overwhelmed by what he feels is life of failures, John is trying desperately to staunch the pain by reclaiming the love interest of his younger years before it is too late and life passes him by.

This is asimple sentence that clearly states the emotional state and stakes of the character and how they drive his actions throughout the script. When looked at with the bullet point reactions to the material and profile, you have a large amount of contextually accurate information on objective and inner life at your disposal. In the next step, we use this information to connect your Castable Type energy and traits to the script to bring the character to life in a way that will bring energy, pace and nuanced behavior to the role.

STEP 3: PRIOR MOMENTS

One of my most influential acting teachers was the brilliant Anna Strasberg. Anna would often say an actor can only prepare for the first moment; anything more is anticipation,which is absolutely correct. When an actor starts a scene or a monologue with the middle or end in mind, or worse, just trying to remember the words, she will have nothing to support her emotionally until she reaches that particular section of the script. The result is an orchestrated delivery of lines. Common examples of this in action are frequent pauses that break the throughline and overly emotional or totally flat delivery of the lines. An actor will either push hard in an attempt to connect or concede the lack of connection and just say the lines. In either case, once the anticipated point is reached, the performance is so off track that the big moment never comes off as planned.

The solution, which is as simple as it is effective, is total immersion in the Prior Moment.

A Prior Moment is just that: the inciting moment prior to a character's entrance, initial action or spoken words on camera or on stage that is propelled by the emotional life and circumstances of the character.

Prior Moments give context, authenticity and energy to what you say and do by investing your mind and body fully in the emotional throughline. Without a rich and textured Prior Moment you have no fuel to support your work.

In audition and monologue situations, a Prior Moment is considered part of the performance. In fact, it is often the only moment when an actor has the undivided attention of the agent or casting director. They are always interested in the behavior and life an actor relates authentically without reliance on words. After a few seconds of hearing lines, most agents and casting directors turn their attention to the headshot and resume you've given them to make a few notes or think about what else they have on their agenda.

With so much riding on the Prior Moment, it is crucial to devote all the time and attention needed to do it well.

Creating a Prior Moment is where technique meets pure imagination. You are not bound strictly by the constraints of the script as this is a moment that takes place inside of the character, before the scene begins. Personalization and specificity are the keys. The goal is to connect yourself to the same emotional and physical place in the throughline as the character you are playing through sensorial awareness. This is often misinterpreted as getting yourself worked up into an emotional state of some sort. The difference may seem semantic but in practice, it is quite distinct. A provoked emotional state is forced, indicated and lacking physical authenticity. It is intellectual and will remain trapped in your head, unable to be expressed in movement and behavior. If you try to get yourself into an emotional state like the feelings of desperation our example character, John, is experiencing, and you focus on the *idea* of being desperate, you will lose that key element once another thought, like hitting your mark or listening for a cue, enters your mind.

From a practical standpoint, it's implausible to think yourself into an emotional state for use in a Prior Moment. Trying to do that is unhealthy psychologically and unreliable creatively. What does work is to experience the tactile elements of that state during the moment prior to your entrance. Think of the emotional state you want to evoke as a deeply-hued color then break it down to its primary components which you can then bring to life. For John, his desperation is born of feelings of failure and running out of time. His failure is the loss of a relationship with the person he loves, who represents his youth.

We now have loss as the emotional state to invoke. There's just one big problem with trying to play loss. Loss is a negative and you cannot play a negative. It is flat, lifeless and un-relatable to the camera and audience. You have to go deeper, to the desire, the want, the need, the active or the *positive*. That is what drives the throughline. John isn't spending the entire script mired in loss, he is trying to get what he believes he wants, his ex-wife. His emotional state and your prior moment is about getting something. He is trying to regain control of his life. Now we have a positive, active choice that can be played. This is definitely not a mere word game. It's getting to the inciting action, the heart of the character.

Even if you had to play a depressed, suicidal role like Jessie Cates in the Marsha Norman play, *'night Mother*, you would find in the character notes that Jessie has finally gained control of her mind and body and is determined to hang on to it for one last night, so she can complete the action which she believes will stop her pain. The role can only be played by honing in on the active and positive even though, for Jessie, that is suicide. Keep this in mind as you determine what needs to be invoked in your Prior Moment.

I had a very talented young girl who came to me for private coaching to prepare for the role of Anne Frank. The actress did not want to play the role because she feared digging into the sadness and loss the of the character's world. I quickly pointed out to her that Anne Frank was filled with hopes and dreams of her future and the desire to be outdoors again, be free and live. That was at the core of her emotional throughline, that was her interior world. The fear and sadness were born of the circumstances of the character's situation. That is not what you live, it's what you react to as the action unfolds. The life created in a Prior Moment, is an active, interior one that is just about to run into the action of the throughline.

This also illustrates how breaking down complicated or difficult emotions into their primary colors allows you to connect to a character whose life doesn't mirror your own. You do not have to be suicidal, a holocaust victim or even a parent or criminal to play one believably. If you can access the same core feelings and motivations, you have the basis of the role.

Once you've chosen what your Prior Moment will consist of, it's time to bring it to life. The best tool for the task is an affective memory. This is a basic exercise in many schools of acting, sometimes called emotional or sense memory. The goal is to connect to the emotional situation of the character by recalling a personal memory that elicits similar feelings. By focusing on the physical aspects of the memory being recalled rather than trying to dredge up emotions from the past, you will get a tangible, relatable connection. When working with a sense memory, the strongest reactions often come from the small, unexpected details. Do not rush through the exercise or force an expected result. Do not feel the need to manipulate a memory to match the script. Make a smart, clear choice and if it doesn't give you what you need, choose a new memory to explore.

Returning to our example role of John, who is trying to *regain* control, you need to experience the tactile elements of a time when you actually felt *out of control* to bottom into the character. The script provides the words and actions for trying to regain control. When I coached an actor through a very similar role he chose to explore his memories of the first time he ever skied. It was a high school field trip and over a decade in the past. When using affective memory, it is best to use events that are at least five years old as the emotions surrounding the event are more settled and reliable to use. He recalled the event as one of breathless fear as he desperately tried to control the skis on an icy slope in biting cold weather. He was sure that a fall would be deadly, even though he was on a beginner's trail. Through the affective memory exercise, he focused on recreating the physical sensation of biting cold wind stinging his face, the pull of the skis on his knees, the whooshing sound in his ears and how cold and dry his mouth felt. He had been screaming open mouthed all the way down and the wind dried his mouth out completely and made his chest feel heavy and tight. Recalling that detail and re-experiencing that sensation sensorially set his hair on end and made his stomach flip flop. He further explored how angry and embarrassed he felt when he got to the bottom of the slope and was teased by his friends. He found what he needed to bring physical authenticity and emotional connection to the role. Incorporating this memory into the moment prior to the start of his monologue, and keeping the tactile sensation of a dry mouth and heavy chest going until his first emotional transition, infused his performance with a unique energy that made it very much his own.

As you consider what to choose as the Prior Moment for each of your Castable Type monologues, do not focus on a perfect situational match. If you get to that *bottomed in* emotional driver, the core want of the character, the right affective memory will be apparent. Keep notes on what you explore physically and the emotions evoked as a result. Do not judge your emotions or the results. Again, simple notes are best, so if your first choice isn't as rich and full as you would like it to be, set it aside and try a new one. By keeping notes, you will be able to revisit the affective memories you have worked on for current and future projects.

STEP 4: COMPLETE THOUGHTS

This is the key step in our technique. It will allow you to master lines and find the right pace without the pitfalls of memorization and falling into vocal patterns and traps.

To understand best how working in Complete Thoughts will transform the quality of your acting its easiest to start with a monologue. Once you have a feel for the technique you will quickly see how it can be applied to passages of dialogue in scenes.

Most actors try to deconstruct a monologue by taking one sentence at a time, breaking it down into fragments or beats and then looking for meaning in every little chunk. The rationale for making these choppy choices is usually punctuation, the way the words are laid out on the page so it's a segment that can be remembered easily. None of this has any bearing on performance.

People do not speak in beats. People speak with the intention of expressing a complete thought. One character wants to get his or her thought across to another character. The thought may be expressed fully and succinctly, interrupted by others or by digressions from the speaker. A person may take a long, circuitous, story-filled route to expressing a thought in whole or in part. That is often the basis of a theatrical monologue. Whether the style is stream of consciousness or linear and spare, the words are said with the intention of expressing a complete thought. Deconstructing a monologue without that understanding will sink an actor's work by disconnecting from the emotional throughline of the story and skewing the authentic intentions of the character.

When you attempt to perform a monologue from beat to beat to beat, the result is akin to being stuck in rush hour traffic. Stops and starts. Hit the gas then slam the brakes. No momentum, sustained energy or understanding of the pace of the script is apparent. It is acting by punctuation, acting based on trying to memorize lines rather than expressing the character's emotions. By pausing after each beat you are inserting a break that requires an emotional transition of some sort in order to move on to the next beat. If an actor is working on a half page-long monologue it could easily result in two dozen pauses, each requiring its own emotional transition to move through the script. If you've taken a serious acting class and watched a fellow actor struggling with a monologue in just this way, you understand how torturous it is to sit through and why it is the antithesis of good acting. You cannot act a series of beats. You cannot act punctuation. Not a comma, period, ellipsis, exclamation point or question mark. The last two come at the end of a sentence: actors should never wait until the end of a sentence or line to *insert* emotion. Try asking a question normally and then asking the same question flatly, acting the question mark at the end to understand this point immediately. Sentence structure and the layout of the words on the page should never be a factor in acting technique. Even with Shakespearean monologues you must understand the thoughts being expressed *first* in order to make use of the clues and elevated language inherent in the meter of the verse, when it is in use. The only time an actor should use a beat is when he needs or is directed to take a momentary pause (which is the definition of a beat in acting) to register a reaction or a thought. This is commonly used with laugh lines, sometimes called zingers. The ability to make that pause or beat full to the point of adding to the comedic effect is really a continuation of the complete thought being expressed in the humor. The beat or pause taken before the zinger is delivered, is words unspoken but communicated physically. Understanding the emotional throughline and how it builds determines how long a beat is taken, how pregnant the pause. That sense of timing with beats either enhances the comedy or kills the humor.

Using Complete Thoughts to deconstruct a monologue will clarify the emotional throughline and the transitions so you can support them with emotional and physical energy through the breath. This will also help you find and maintain an optimal pace and stay out of bad actor habits that undercut your talent and get your headshots tossed in the trash.

To begin, find the complete thoughts in the monologue. Keep in mind that most monologues have just a few. Ignore all punctuation. Toss sentence structure out the window. This is a single but crucial step in this acting technique. Let the emotional throughline of your character be your guide, not the typeset. Since many of the smartest actors are also great readers who have a difficult time ignoring the signals of punctuation, I recommend strongly retyping monologues without punctuation or taking a white out pen to your script so your eyes are not drawn to these marks.

If we continue with our character John, we know he is feeling out of control. The action of the storyline is comprised of his attempts to regain control. With that in mind, look over his monologue and break it down into Complete Thoughts:

JOHN: *I need to borrow some money. I gotta take a little road trip and I need cash for gas. I gotta leave now. I don't have time to waste. I'll pay you back next week as soon as I cash my paycheck, okay? I'll throw in an extra twenty for interest. I just have to get on the road now. I'm trying to get to a wedding . . . it's a family affair and I can't miss it. You won't believe who it is that's getting married, either. It's my wife. My wife. My ex-wife. She's getting married to this guy and . . . I . . . can't be late. I can't miss the start of the ceremony. I wasn't actually invited but you know who was? My brother! My stinking brother! He actually called me and asked if he was supposed to bring a gift. My brother called me to ask if he should bring a gift to my wife's wedding to some guy she just met. He wanted to know since he bought us a gift when we got married if he needed to buy something again. Like he had put out for one toaster in his lifetime and he didn't want to do it again. I didn't know what to say. I just hung up. She left the toaster when she left me so what the hell does she need with another toaster anyway? Obviously she has no interest in toast. I guess I could have asked him to pick me up but it's too late for that now. The ceremony starts in a few hours so I gotta hit the road if I'm going to get there. I just need some cash for gas. Anything you can spare. I'll pay you back with interest."*

There is no absolute right or wrong choices with Complete Thoughts. The choices you make must work well and be true to the throughline of the character and script. If they don't, scrap them and try new choices. The ability to make choices in this step will become faster and more intuitive as you gain more practice with the technique. When I look at this monologue from the point of view of John, I hear him communicating three Complete Thoughts:

1. *I need to borrow some money. I gotta take a little road trip and I need cash for gas. I gotta leave now. I don't have time to waste. I'll pay you back next week as soon as I cash my paycheck, okay? I'll throw in an extra twenty for interest. I just have to get on the road now. I'm trying to get to a wedding . . . it's a family affair and I can't miss it.*

2. *You won't believe who it is that's getting married either. It's my wife. My wife. My ex-wife. She's getting married to this guy and . . . I . . . can't be late. I can't miss the start of the ceremony. I wasn't actually invited but you know who was? My brother! My stinking brother! He actually called me and asked if he was supposed to bring a gift. My brother called me to ask if he should bring a gift to my wife's wedding to some guy she just met. He wanted to know since he bought us a gift when we got married if he needed to buy something again. Like he had put out for one toaster in his*

*lifetime and he didn't want to do it again. I didn't know what
to say. I just hung up. She left the toaster when she left me
so what the hell does she need with another toaster anyway.
Obviously she has no interest in toast.*

3. *I guess I could have asked him to pick me up but it's too
late for that now. The ceremony starts in a few hours so I gotta
hit the road if I'm going to get there. just need some cash for
gas. Anything you can spare. I'll pay you back with interest.*

Each thought is complete in its own way. The first is asking
for help with his problem. The second is explaining how he's
on the outside looking in or how he is lacking control over
the situation and wants to regain it. The digression about his
brother and the toaster is not a new thought, merely his way
of illustrating how out of control the situation is for him at the
moment. The third Complete Thought is about trying to find
a solution. These are three very distinct Complete Thoughts
once you see them separated on the page. If you treat the entire
monologue as one thought, one emotion, one color, you will
lose emotional clarity and the nuanced inflection and behavior
that comes with it. If performed as one thought, the monologue
becomes a diatribe rather than insight into the heart and mind of
the character. When you connect to and support each thought,
you allow your Castable Type energy and unique personality traits to infuse the moments of nuance and bring out the
subtleties and life experiences of the character. You inhabit the
character and start to own the role.

Think for a moment of an event in your own life that
could be told as a monologue. Go back in time to your first
day of school. Think about how you would relate that event
in words to an audience. It seems like one simple story, but
within the tale you will have several complete thoughts that
you will want to get across to your listeners, each one with
its own emotional meaning that contributes to the whole by
giving life to each element of the monologue. Wash your story
in one color and it loses its life and impact. It loses you.

Once you have your monologue's Complete Thoughts

delineated, give each an *action phrase* from the speaker's point of view. Not a sentence, just a phrase that is positive/ active which exemplifies the thought. For John's monologue, my *Complete Thought Phrases* are:

1. Help me out
2. I want control
3. I have a plan

Each phrase is simple, clean, and clearly active. Anything more complex, negative or passive will trip you up.

Next, look within each Complete Thought for a few *key words* in the script to support your Complete Thought phrase. My *Key Word* choices are:

1. *"don't have time to waste"*
2. *"can't miss the start"*
3. *"hit the road"*

Your action phrase is what you should be thinking before speaking the Complete Thought. The key words are the crux of the thought that needs to be stressed in order to insure your meaning is driven home. Before I explain how to put this step of the technique into practice, there is one more element to cover: Breathing.

To put your Complete Thought work into action, you need to connect it to supporting, energizing breaths. Breathing is the conduit for two key components of performance, relaxation and connection. When the instrument, the term used for the actor's physical being, is relaxed yet energized, emotion can travel freely through the body and be effectively expressed.

The importance of breathing in performance is not to be underestimated. The quickest and easiest way to grasp this is to watch *and* listen to an actor say a line or two from a monologue, breathing in deeply and fully before speaking so that the breath energizes and supports the emotional life under the words. Then, have the actor do the same lines without breathing in before speaking. The flat, lifeless performance of the unsupported, second reading consists of the very same words as the first, yet the first one will look and sound infinitely better.

When you don't breathe you are frozen like a deer in headlights. Holding, contracting or limiting your breath literally freezes your instrument. Your emotions are trapped inside of your body. You have nothing to propel you along the throughline. That is why actors who don't breathe have to force their emotions, take odd pauses or manipulate and stutter over words in an attempt to generate a sense of momentum. Without emotional connection and the energy that comes with it, the actor has to resort to tricks and indication to push through the material. Forcing emotional connection will make faces turn red, fingers clench, throats tighten and nerve induced physical behaviors overtake the actor. Breathing, by contrast, will relax the instrument, connect the emotional and physical, making everything work.

Each Complete Thought phrase requires you to breathe correctly. That means deep, full natural inhalations and exhalations. This is not Lamaze, spaghetti or box breathing, blowing, puffing or anything to do with a vocal warm up. It's just breathing. In through your nose and out through your nose and mouth as you speak. Don't hold, measure or meter your breath. Think of one breath as one burst of energy supporting and expressing one Complete Thought. As you inhale fully, think about your Complete Thought Phrase. As you say the lines of that thought, let the words come out on the exhalation. As the thought is expressed and completed, the words and breath should be completed as well. Use the Key Words you selected within the thought as a marker while developing the monologue. Those are the words you have determined express the crux of the Complete Thought. As you allow the words to come out on the breath, try to give noticeable emphasis to or hit only the key words and nothing else. This helps you stay true to the thought and begin to develop the appropriate pace by imprinting the core meaning of the thought in your instrument. Once hit, consciously release your remaining breath and let the rest of words in the thought simply tumble out with it. Be aware that releasing is not rushing. It is as if you have gotten your point across and can now wrap up your point and let go of the thought as you let go of the remaining breath.

To put Complete Thoughts supported by energizing breathing into practice, use this simple exercise:

Begin by standing naturally and breathing in deeply and fully through the nose, rising up on your toes and opening your arms wide so you can feel your core expanding. Hold the air in for a moment or two then exhale as completely as possible through the mouth while lowering your arms and weight on to your feet. Repeat this ten times at an even, relaxed yet energized pace. Expand your core more on each inhale and push more air out on the exhale each time. Use this to connect physically and mentally to the energy and power that travels through you on the breath.

Next, add in the words of the monologue. With script in hand, look at your Complete Thought phrases and Key Words. Substitute the phrase for the actual lines of the complete thought, leaving only the Key Words in the place they were written. For example, our first complete thought goes from this:

>*I need to borrow some money. I gotta take a little road trip and I need cash for gas. I gotta leave now. I don't have time to waste. I'll pay you back next week as soon as I cash my paycheck, okay? I'll throw in an extra twenty for interest. I just have to get on the road now. I'm trying to get to a wedding . . . its a . . . family affair and I can't miss it.*

To this:

>*help me out help me out help me out* I don't have time to waste *help me out help me out help me out help me out*

Remember to breathe in fully before you begin speaking and support the words with the breath. Do not collapse your chest or shoulders or keep them locked in place. Speak your Complete Thought Phrase with the meaning and intention it holds but not the actual words of the script. Connect instead to the clear, concise words of your phrase, in this case, "help me out." When you reach your Key Words, which you have selected, give them the most emphasis, then consciously release the energy of the Complete Thought by exhaling as you say the remaining words. The goal is to have expressed the emotion by way of the breath and the words at the same time so that there is nothing left. The point has been made by the character. You can then move on to the next, new Complete Thought in the same way, unencumbered by the previous emotional color. This lets you go deeper into the emotional throughline with more energy and lightness of technique. It is in those moments of transition, between each of the Complete Thoughts, that you will be able to bring your Castable Type traits to the role with nuanced behavior that fuses you with the character.

If we return to those key words you are now hitting within the Complete Thought, you will find that what you must absolutely emphasize to get the character's point across is what sets the pace of delivery. I want to remind you that, at this stage in the technique, the purpose is building a fully developed Castable Type character and role. This is the middle step, not the final step. We are finding pace by clarifying the emotion and need the character is trying to express. Using key words you have chosen infuses your personality into the character's emotional life while still being very true to the intention of the script. At the same time, it employs the text as a tool for imprinting the throughline in your mind and body. When practiced correctly, this eliminates the need for memorization by rote.

Continue the exercise by adding back pieces of the actual text until you are using the text as written. Use your script while doing this. The purpose is to connect to the emotions of the character, not to drill for memorization. Go thought to thought. If you find you are losing your connection by holding or metering your breath, start over from the beginning of the Complete Thought. Don't imprint or ingrain mistakes into your work.

Be sure to give yourself plenty of time to exhale fully, completing the thought and expending the energy that goes with it. Don't rush the exhale or stop exhaling if you run out of words in that thought. Complete the emotional expression by completing the exhalation. There is emotional life in that last bit of breath and it is crucial to let it out. Exhaling, which is expressing and relating, is the part of this technique that many actors have the hardest time mastering. The moments between the thoughts are the times when an actor is essentially naked on stage or in front of the camera. When there are no scripted words to say, no mannerisms to fall back on, when you have to simply *be* in that moment, is the opportunity to own the role. This technique allows you to find those moments and live in them with authenticity. Don't rush through it. Don't fear expression. It is the essence of the art of acting.

When I introduce new coaching clients to Complete Thought work I am amazed by how many get tripped up simply breathing. It's the one thing we all learned to do the moment our bottoms got spanked in the delivery room, yet I see all manner of bizarre breathing from actors who seem hell-bent on finding something to make into a major issue when developing a working technique. There is no acting technique in which full and connected breathing is not a core component. Often I am told by an actor that he or she is running out of breath and cannot possibly get all the words in the Complete Thought out before asphyxiating. Uh-huh. My icy response to such utter nonsense goes like this: if I was a psycho killer trying to drown you in the toilet, how many seconds would I need to hold your head in the bowl of water before you stopped kicking and screaming? You can cue the *Jeopardy!* music here because the actor will always stop to think seriously about a reply. The answer is between 90 seconds and three minutes, an amount of time that is far longer than most audition monologues and commercials, let alone a Complete Thought. You and I have more than enough air in our lungs to support and energize the verbal and physical expression of a Complete Thought without speed talking, turning blue, waving our arms or passing out. If you feel, after breathing in fully, you don't have enough air to express and support a Complete Thought, you are blocked by mental tension that is manifesting itself physically. The solution is to relax by *breathing through it* and verbally releasing the tension on the exhalation. Yes, the answer is Complete Thought breathing. Funny how that works out!

The second, big benefit to this technique is that it will help you find the perfect pace for delivering your lines. When you work with Complete Thoughts supported by the breath you move beyond punctuation and vocal patterns. You are, instead, guided by the emotional throughline. Moving from thought to thought, just as the character does, takes you out of your head and into his or hers. You now have a clear emotional point to get across even if the character is not articulate or digresses. You understand with perfect clarity why seemingly random thoughts have meaning to the character and need to be said at that moment in time. As with Clean Readings, it is another technique for understanding the whole in context and not getting sidetracked by overanalyzing lines.

Step 5: Layering

To this point, we've been connecting the role to you. Now, with the text and throughline completely clear and a personalized physical and emotional connection alive in your instrument, it's time to connect you to the role by Layering in additional elements of the character and script in your monologue. This will give added depth to your performance while tying your work in with the production or concept as a whole.

The elements you should consider for inclusion will vary from piece to piece. There is no set formula to follow. All layers have meaning, but the material determines what is truly required by the actor. What is crucial is that this step of our technique should always come after the development of Prior Moment and Complete Thought work. Form follows function, in that steps two and three give specificity and clarity to the character's intention, purpose and place. In this step, Layering, style and dimension are now added to further shape the performance.

As you Layer in the appropriate stylistic elements, your singular emphasis on the Key Words of your Complete Thoughts will soften slightly and blend in more with the rest of the text. Just be careful to not lose the clarity they have brought to your performance. Stylistic elements should enhance the energy and subtleties you discovered in steps two and three and give physical structure to nuanced behavior.

The major elements that you should examine and add into your work include:

Genre and style of the material

At the 1904 premiere of *The Cherry Orchard* at the Moscow Art Theater, playwright Anton Chekhov was said to be upset over Konstantin Stanislavski's direction of his play. The great Stanislavski had staged it as a tragedy when Chekhov considered his work a comedy. Even the masters of the form can go astray. They can get away with it but you and I can't.

It is absolutely crucial to have an understanding of the style and genre of the material you are working on, either as written or as conceived by the director. When working on Castable Type monologues, you have the latitude to make adjustments to the material to best suit your needs but will still need to demonstrate your comprehension of the work as the writer conceived it. An important factor in choosing Castable Types monologues is showcasing your ease and expertise with particular styles of writing and genres of work for which you are well suited. One would never approach the work of absurdist master Christopher Durang the same as that of David Mamet, master of the *f-bomb*. Both are contemporary writers of incredible precision, not only with words but with the sound of and logic behind the dialogue they craft. Both require performances be driven by intense psychological forces that are much deeper than the words, which are often cutting, shocking and brutal on their own. The style of delivery, sense of reality and the characters who inhabit these stories are vastly different. Durang often requires a frenzied level of physical energy that elicits laughter and broad move-

75

ment which at times seems dreamlike and at other moments, almost burlesque. Mamet tends to be smoldering, ready to explode physically without getting to that point, creating a sense of tension that is as seductive as it is unsettling. Even when comparing the work of two non-linear, absurdist writers like Durang and, one of my personal favorites, Naomi Iizuka, there are significant differences in style, tone and physical life of the plays.

Reading and viewing plays and film, along with research of the writer and his or her influences will give you the base knowledge required to identify and play genre and style. I've included a reading list at the end of this book that will help build your expertise in this area.

Incorporating the requirements of genre and style into your work will affect language, diction, movement —especially with blocking and staging. It will not change the need for honest and personal connection to the emotional throughline of the role you are creating. It simply adds a layer of physical behaviors and informs the pace of delivery of the lines. The core of your character should remain rooted in the solid foundation of his or her inner life as you realize it in your Complete Thought work.

Researching the character and scripted behaviors

If you're working on a period piece, an historical character, one from a very specific region or have to perform actions requiring a dedicated skill set, you must research these layers to portray them authentically. While that may seem obvious if you are supposed to handle a weapon, diaper a baby, play the role of a surgeon or greet the king, it can extend out into your monologue in unexpected ways. Finding these moments of truth and authentic detail can raise your work to an even higher level of quality.

One of the first roles I ever had to research was assigned to me in my first semester as a drama student at NYU. The role was Chrissy, a stripper, in David Rabe's *In the Boom Boom Room*. The instruction from my acting teacher was to take a male friend along for safety and head to Times Square to check out the peep shows and go-go bars, making notes on the atmosphere, demeanor of the women who worked in these establishments and reactions of the men who patronized them. This would help me understand the self-loathing and trauma that drove the naive and often violated Chrissy to accept willingly such degrading conditions. I would have seen the emotional bubble the dancers used for protection, the lack of direct eye contact except when money was exchanged and the way the ladies slipped in and out of their sexualized personas as needed. I would have understood all this *if* I had gotten inside of one of those dank, neon palaces. When I approached the doors with my bodyguard buddy, who was in his Adam Ant phase and was wearing more lipgloss than the dancers, entry was refused by every bouncer we met. I guess I should have left my binder, notebook and highlighters at home and tried to fit in a little more. I never did master the role or even get a handle on the character. As much as I intellectually understood her, I had no authentic behavioral elements to bring Chrissy's world to life. I didn't get to uncover the one or two details in context that would have connected me to a *Boom Boom Room* world at a professional level.

As I've written earlier, you don't have to be an abused, sexually confused stripper to portray one effectively. But in this instance, I didn't have any reference points or even a visual idea of what the character's world was truly like so I could add that necessary layer into my work. This was back in the early 80's, long before cardio pole-dancing was offered at gyms and walking around Times Square late at night with a glam rock body guard was asking for trouble. Which points out another factor that may require research, era. I'm sharing this particular story because recently I coached an actor who was auditioning for the role of Chrissy in a revival of this very play. She couldn't comprehend that not so long ago, working as an exotic dancer was a reason for social scorn and personal shame. This actress had thought of it as a just another job option for fit, fearless females, which it definitely was not at the time the play was written. She needed to research the era of the play as well as the world of strip clubs at that time to succeed where I failed so many years earlier.

Never assume that if you have the blocking, business or a visual of the setting, you will always be able to bring the world of your character to life or believably perform specific, scripted behaviors. You may know how to play the piano but not be aware of what it looks and feels like to play a Steinway at Carnegie Hall if you are portraying a classical concert pianist. Classes in historical styles are *de rigueur* for actors as is the ability to research time periods, technical skill sets, manners and cultural regions beyond the act of typing a few key words into a search engine. The scripted behaviors and world of your character are most often a physical layer to add to your performance. Choosing a physical action or activity gleaned from your research and doing it during your Complete Thought work is the most effective way to weave layered elements into your Castable Type Monologue and performance.

Interviews and viewing are other methods of research. Getting the story first hand, even if you are watching interviews via video, can give you an intimate understanding of how situations and events effect behaviors and emotions in ways you may have never imagined. While working with an actor on the role of Carter in Neil LaBute's *Fat Pig*, I asked him to seek out first-hand accounts of growing up with a morbidly obese, food addicted mother, to gain insight into the apparent cruelty of the character toward fat women. The actor was in high demand with lots of bookings so we had limited time to work on the part. Watching video interviews of children who grew up with food addicted moms helped him quickly understand that it wasn't just social embarrassment that drove his character but feelings of alienation, being ignored coupled with jealousy and anger at the food that consumed the mother's existence. My client first thought Carter's cruelty was driven by shallow concerns over physical beauty but there was a deep wound festering inside him. This insight gave the actor so much more to work with and yielded a far more compelling performance.

Relationship to other characters

Your character's relationship to others in the script is an area ripe for exploration. Characters who are core components of your emotional throughline are related to through the wants and needs you have already covered in the Prior Moment and Complete Thought steps. In Layering, you can address the people your character interacts with more incidentally. A beautiful pair of examples of this are found in one of my all-time favorite films, *The Trip to Bountiful*. If you are one of my private students or in my Acting for Film Workshop, you will study this movie. It is a master class in acting. The main character, Carrie Watts, played to perfection by a luminous Geraldine Page, encounters a woman on a bus and a sheriff on her journey home to Bountiful. She has no history with either of these people, no established relationship. She knows she will never see these people again, yet her interaction with each furthers the plot by exposing the inner life of Carrie and more of her history, motivations and behaviors. Carrie must connect with them on an immediate and authentic basis. In the case of the woman on the bus, it is for solace and companionship which turns into empathy and affection. With the sheriff, it is for help and information, which becomes a chance for Carrie to demonstrate that she is not an overwrought, foolish old woman. Through their interaction, she regains a measure of self-respect and centeredness.

To fully realize all that the writers hope to expose through these scenes, you must be living in the emotional throughline of your character so fully that simple moment to moment specificity will carry you through believably. You must also be listening so you can receive and react to everything another character brings to the action. When the moment to moment nature of the encounter touches on a nerve, you will then be able to feel it and let it affect your character in the context in which it was written then respond with authenticity. It may be a moment that changes your character or simply a device for exposition. In either case, the way in which you relate to these other characters can only be driven by the Prior Moment work you bring to the scene and the truth of the moment to moment life you live on stage or in front of the camera.

When working with actors on this layer, I take them out of the studio to a public place to improvise a scene based on the monologue. Being in Manhattan, we make use of the stores and parks nearby. The actors must talk and respond to me using only the words of their monologue. I can interject comments or respond to what is said as well as whatever may be going on around us. This environmental immersion helps the actors solidify their Complete Thought work while expanding it to include truly listening and reacting to another character and surroundings. The actor with whom I was working with on the role of Carter in *Fat Pig* walked through a department store with me for 20 minutes, only able to speak his harsh lines about Carter's obese mother. The exercise, though short, had instant results. The actor was immediately aware of how other shoppers reacted to him as they overheard his words and how hard he had to work to get his point across to me, while I looked at merchandise and we both interacted with sales associates. His Complete Thoughts became even clearer as he had to make me listen and understand. His delivery became more nuanced as he felt the cruelty, hurt and anger emerge in his character and the judgment of me and anyone who caught a few moments of what he said. Environmental exercises are an effective way to add in a relationship layer to other characters connected to your Castable Type Monologue.

Secondary intentions and story arcs

It's a common component of many scripts, especially comedies, to have a secondary story arc to the main one, weaving in and out of the action before tying in at the dénouement. Often this a running gag that serves as a point of humor or character development or, in dramas, a person who is able to contribute to the final resolution in some way though he or she may not have been deeply involved in the plot. These characters and story arcs are easy to spot in screwball comedies or Woody Allen movies. They are staples of crime dramas. Think of the witness or expert who helps to solve the mystery. You should approach these layers of your performance in much the same way as you would an encounter with other characters as described above. The main difference to keep in mind is that these layers are usually more physical and related to place and setting. That requires your Prior Moment work be focused on place and the physical to an even stronger degree. What you take away from that Prior Moment may be a simple, less emotional physical reaction but enough to propel your moment to moment work through the secondary intention or minor story arc truthfully and energetically.

Step 6: Performance Level

The final step in our technique is to take your Castable Type monologues to the same finished quality expected at a performance or shoot.

Every professional actor must learn to get his or her work to Performance Level. Each time you perform, your work must be as polished, unselfconscious and energized as possible. This includes auditions. Every audition is an opportunity to show your Performance Level work. Nobody wants to watch you at fifty percent of your best. You won't even make it to the call back. All the elements explored and mastered as you use this technique to develop the role should flow together seamlessly by the completion of this step. Performance Level work has a physical life as well as an interior, emotional life; a history and context that distinguishes it from less experienced class or studio quality work. To achieve this you must have total connection to the character, complete concentration and energy to sustain the performance as well

81

as a degree of ease and comfort with the role so that you live it, even when not speaking lines. It means infusing the part with your own Castable Type energy and nuanced behavior. Too many actors want to demonstrate how hard they're working at a role or how many technical elements they can include in their work. This workmanlike approach that tries to advertise your talent rather than use it serves no purpose. All the hard work and technique should, ultimately, become so enmeshed, so natural that you are one with the character and simply alive. Your acting technique should be effortless and invisible. That way, your unique take on the role, your personality, your Castable Type can shine through.

To get your work to its exciting Performance Level you will need to complete the previous five steps of our technique so you are grounded and solidly connected to the character. You should be ready to take ownership of the role. That is the goal. The way to do it is to bring these two final elements to your creation.

Define the emotional transitions

Between each Complete Thought is an emotional transition. In Step Four, I defined the emotional energy before and after each transition. Now, it's time to define the transition. That is done by writing the line between the lines, one sentence or phrase that connects the Complete Thoughts in a way that makes perfect sense to your character as realized by your Castable Type, one sentence that becomes the script for the emotional transition.

This line is not an addition to the actual spoken script. You aren't usurping the job of writer. It's from the inner monologue of the character as only your Castable Type plays it. It is said only as you work through this sixth and final step. When it's time to walk in front of the camera or the audience, it should be fully internalized and not spoken out loud.

We do this now, rather than as a part of the Complete Thought work for three reasons. First, because we are deconstructing the actual script in Step Four to gain clarity and connection to the emotional throughline and bottom into the character. We want to stay with the script and mine everything it has to offer us at that point.

Second, in Step Five, Layering, we are adding in script-based, non-dialogue elements of the role that have a profound effect on the behavior, interior and exterior life of the character. Depending on the vehicle, that is crucial information to incorporate, especially as it relates to the genre and style of the production. It needs to be blended into the work before we take full ownership of the role.

Lastly, it is at this final step that we fully develop the physical life and use the line between the lines as our springboard to do it.

Returning to our example monologue, we can see our Complete Thought work so far, with the Complete Thought Phrases written before each thought and the Key Words highlighted in bold:

Complete Thought Phrase: Help me out

1. *I need to borrow some money. I gotta take a little road trip and I need cash for gas. I gotta leave now.* **I don't have time to waste.** *I'll pay you back next week as soon as I cash my paycheck, okay? I'll throw in an extra twenty for interest. I just have to get on the road now. I'm trying to get to a wedding . . . it's a family affair and I can't miss it.*

Complete Thought Phrase: I want control

2. *You won't believe who it is that's getting married either. It's my wife. My wife. My ex-wife. She's getting married to this guy and . . . I . . . can't be late.* **I can't miss the start** *of the ceremony. I wasn't actually invited but you know who was? My brother! My stinking brother! He actually called me and asked if he was supposed to bring a gift. My brother called me to ask if he should bring a gift to my wife's wedding to some guy she just met. He wanted to know since he bought us a gift when we got married if he needed to buy something again. Like he had put out for one toaster in his lifetime and*

83

he didn't want to do it again. I didn't know what to say. I just hung up. She left the toaster when she left me so what the hell does she need with another toaster anyway? Obviously she has no interest in toast.

Complete Thought Phrase: I have a plan

3. *I guess I could have asked him to pick me up but it's too late for that now. The ceremony starts in a few hours so I gotta **hit the road** if I'm going to get there. I just need some cash for gas. Anything you can spare. I'll pay you back with interest.*

Let your Castable Type do the talking for you. Allow the part of you that most strongly identifies with your monologue character add in the lines that become the connective tissue. These are the lines that your character says in his head to take him from one thought to the next, the lines that allow the words written by someone else to make perfect, personal sense.

My choices are:

1. **Don't make me beg, okay, I feel like dirt already.**
2. **Nobody else gets it but I know what I'm doing, I can fix this.**

To incorporate these lines, run through your monologue as you have been doing using Complete Thoughts energized by the full inhalation of the breath to support and energize the emotional life, emphasizing your key words before releasing the rest of the thought on the exhalation. Between the exhalation/completion of the first thought and the inhalation/start of the second thought, say your newly written line. Do not energize it with a Complete Thought breath. Instead, *move* as you say it. Let the physical action be the source of energy and support for the line. Make it a clean, clear physical movement which makes sense to you as you speak the line. Examples of this may be getting up from or sitting down on a chair, crossing to a window to look out or closing the curtain to block the light, punching the air (rather than throwing an object in frustration), dropping your head in your hands, flopping on to the sofa or jumping for joy. Whatever your choice, keep it simple and straightforward: a physical manifestation of the feelings being expressed by the line you have written. Do not make it a series of movements or intricately detailed blocking.

In Step Four you should have been running the lines of your monologue while using the script to imprint your breathing in muscle memory and your Complete Thoughts and Key words in your emotional memory. By the end of that process, most actors have the lines fully integrated and can easily go off book. Adding in your newly created lines between the lines will put you back on the page as you should write them down and use the script to stay on point. There are no bonus points to be won for getting off book when you are best served by using it. Your script is a tool to help you get the job done properly and accurately. Don't be afraid of making use of it here as you will be able to put it down in very short order.

Our example script will now look like this:

Complete Thought Phrase: **Help me out**

1. *I need to borrow some money. I gotta take a little road trip and I need cash for gas. I gotta leave now.* **I don't have time to waste.** *I'll pay you back next week as soon as I cash my paycheck, okay? I'll throw in an extra twenty for interest. I just have to get on the road now. I'm trying to get to a wedding . . . it's a family affair and I can't miss it.*
Don't make me beg, okay, I feel like dirt already.

Complete Thought Phrase: **I want control**

2. *You won't believe who it is that's getting married either. It's my wife. My wife. My ex-wife. She's getting married to this guy and . . . I . . . can't be late. I* **can't miss the start** *of the ceremony. I wasn't actually invited but you know who was? My brother! My stinking brother! He actually called me and asked if he was supposed to bring a gift. My brother called me to ask if he should bring a*

gift to my wife's wedding to some guy she just met. He wanted to know since he bought us a gift when we got married if he needed to buy something again. Like he had put out for one toaster in his lifetime and he didn't want to do it again. I didn't know what to say. I just hung up. She left the toaster when she left me so what the hell does she need with another toaster anyway. Obviously she has no interest in toast.

Nobody else gets it but I know what I'm doing, I can fix this.

Complete Thought Phrase: **I have a plan**

3. *I guess I could have asked him to pick me up but it's too late for that now. The ceremony starts in a few hours so I gotta* **hit the road** *if I'm going to get there. I just need some cash for gas. Anything you can spare. I'll pay you back with interest.*

Our transition lines sit between thoughts 1 and 3. They don't necessarily slow the pace down because they *are* the actual emotional transition. By making the emotional transition physically active, we create a springboard for the Complete Thought we are transitioning into on the inhalation. While this explanation reads in a very technical way, in practice, this is as easy and natural as can be. To get this newly defined transition imprinted into your muscle and emotional memory, just run it. First speaking the line between the lines out loud as you rehearse the monologue, then incorporating the movement into that transition line. After a number of run-throughs in this manner, say the line as part of your inner monologue rather than out loud but continue doing the physical movement at the same time. If you feel as though you are losing the clarity of the transition or rushing the physical movement without words, alternate doing the line silently and out loud. After several run-throughs, you will find that you can keep the transition fully defined without speaking the added words and the movement will help you more fully inhale and exhale the breath. The physical movement you added with the now silent transition line will become fully realized, nuanced behavior, giving external life to your internal feelings; or, as the casting folks like to say, relating to the camera and the audience.

Yippee!

Directorial detail

The last element to add to your Castable Type monologue and take your work to that all important Performance Level is to add in the details that a good director would if you had one working with you in rehearsal.

While many of the best directors are also trained actors, not every actor can direct or self direct. But every actor can think like a director. That thought process is what we will use to give detailed authenticity to your Castable Type monologue.

Every director has a concept of their production, be it commercial, play, video or film. It is the overall vision of what the project will look, feel and sound like. You too have a concept with your Castable Types as realized on the vision board you started when discovering and defining them. Now you can add to your board the visuals that embody the production concept for your monologue. Since our goal is to have multiple monologues to use for each Castable Type, create a vision board specifically for each of your monologues. The board or page you create will go into your Castable Type guidebook and be of more value than you can imagine at auditions and callbacks. Actors are visual and need tangible reference points to refer to that focus the mind and trigger creative flow. Trying to keep all the details and elements of your work in your mind, while prepping for a cold reading is never going to serve you well. Fleshing out your personal production concept by creating a vision board is one of the more fun actions you can take to improve your work and is a key tool for directors.

Next, a director must address the opening moment of a scene or shot. Actors do this on an emotional level through the Prior Moment. In Step Three, place was a core component in creating your Prior Moment. Now we will revisit place to add the first directorial detail, the opening moment.

When you added your Prior Moment to the monologue, the focus was on how the elements of the moment incited the words and actions of your character in connection to the throughline, yet your Prior Moment contains much more detail than that alone —specifically, place. The place, including the time that your monologue is set has emotional and physical qualities that bring tremendous context to the all-important first moments of your work. They give you the material to add in physical details of the back story like time of day, temperature, season, how the clothing worn effects the character, where the character has come from and how he or she feels about the current place. If you are working with a stand-alone monologue, say one pulled from a collection, utilize elements of the place from your emotional memory exercise.

Treat the opening of your monologue like it's your entrance on the set, even if the selection comes from the middle of a scene or is part of a much longer piece. Improvise your entrance as an exercise of discovery. Feel all the relevant details in-depth and for as long as it takes to experience them. You will then be able to carry these physical and emotional details into the opening moments of the monologue and allow them to flavor the ensuing thoughts and actions. The discoveries made in the exploration of your Prior Moment and entrance improvisation are directly applicable to your monologue and are easily adapted to suit the many different formats in which you will use your piece.

Once the scene or monologue is underway, a director will need to work out the action of the scene, through blocking and/or camera shots. Since we are working on monologues, we will start off with blocking. While most on-camera auditions are done with actors standing on marks, that is not the optimal way to approach this work from the actor's perspective. Just as defining transitions required the addition of material so that it crucial details could be incorporated and then the externals slowly dropped, we will take the same path with blocking.

You will already have added behaviors through the movement of your transition lines and a fully fleshed-out entrance that gives context through the elements of place. Using your vision board and any directions given in the script, make a simple line drawing of your set. Think about movements your character needs to make to fulfill necessary tasks written into the script. Consider actions you feel your character would do in the script. Keep it to what is really necessary. It may be as simple as walking into the room and looking out the window or putting on a jacket before exiting. Walk through this blocking as you run your Complete Thoughts, keeping the behavioral actions you have already added and using them as a guide. Only block in what you need to do to take you from behavior to behavior, along with anything that may be an absolute requirement of the script. This should keep it simple. Remember that it is usually best to move through your blocking as you are saying the lines. Try to keep the words and actions together. If you find that you are trying frantically to fit in more blocked actions than the script can support, eliminate the excess. Connect your entrance to the blocking as you run through your Complete Thoughts.

Directors pride themselves on attention to detail that rings with authenticity and character exposition. That is already present in your nuanced behaviors but can be further added to your Castable Type monologue through selectively chosen business. If you are unfamiliar with the term business, here is a working definition: blocking is the directed movement the actor makes on the set or stage. This includes entrances, exits, crossing the set, sitting down at the table, getting out of bed and getting dressed, etc. Business is the small detailed actions that flesh out the blocking. For instance, an actor may have her entrance into the waiting room of the dentist's office blocked out as walking through the door, nodding at the receptionist and crossing stage left to have a seat in the waiting area. The director may then ask her to do some business with the magazines on the waiting room table. That would mean interacting with the magazines by selecting one off the table, looking at the cover, leafing through the pages then pausing here and there to look at what's inside. The director won't block out each movement or the amount of time she lingers on the pages of the magazine unless it is key to the script in some way. The actor is expected to be able to look natural, like she is really glancing at the magazines and keep the business going until her next blocked movement or the end of the scene. That's business.

Consider any potential moments of business in your blocked monologue. Are there actions or behaviors you are doing that would be strengthened by more careful attention to detail? Even something as simple as the manner in which a curtain is opened to look out the window can communicate a great deal about your character. The way an action or activity is performed shows demeanor. Traits we used earlier to define Castable Types. Is the demeanor of your character infused with that of your Castable Type? If not, this is your opportunity to add in a degree of detailed demeanor through business to the blocking or physical behavior that makes the role your own.

Finally, just as a director will consider carefully the manner in which a scene ends we, too, will add an ending. a *Post* Moment, if you will, that keeps the energy, action and connection alive even though the words have ended.

Many actors have the extremely bad habit of speaking the last word of the script and then immediately turning to the coach, director or auditioner for some sort of reaction or nod of approval. It is as infuriating to watch as it is self-defeating to the actor. The last word doesn't signal the end. The actor doesn't get to signal the end or call cut. Professional actors do not drop the action to look at someone for notes. It's the sign of a rookie. If you are in this habit or, the grade school version of it where kids say "scene" so we all know the great work has concluded, knock it off!

The Post Moment is the second opportunity you have to hold an auditioner's attention with the focus all on you, rather than the script or copy. It's a second look, a follow up, a chance to make a final impression. You should never waste it by cutting it short or turning it into a plea for approval of your work. Instead, use it to show you've staked claim to the role by keeping that energized connection to the throughline.

Using the Complete Thought Technique teaches you that each thought, each burst of energy which is supported by a connected breath, needs to be fully expressed before moving on to the next thought. Once this step in the technique is mastered, you realize quickly that there is an emotional transition that occurs at the moment of completion. Rather than making a full transition into the new or next thought, live the moment of completion. Experience it. Stand in it and allow it to breathe. Let your audience know there will be another moment in the life of the character. Once you have done that, you can break the proverbial fourth wall and return to your own smiling, professional self.

PUTTING A RIBBON ON IT

Now, with the final ingredients added to take your work to Performance Level, you must rehearse your Castable Type monologues in the same way you would at dress rehearsals of a play or if the camera were rolling, full out, with every aspect of all six steps engaged, making use of every bit of your talent. By working it carefully and thoroughly, the Complete Thought Technique will bring your Castable Types to life through a total connection to a character you play better than the competition. You will now have a vehicle to showcase your talent and let industry decision-makers know how they can make use of that talent in projects that suit you well.

We've used monologues as a means to develop and define your Castable Types and acquire a reliable, proven acting technique to bring your work to the Professional Level required to book professional jobs. The Castable Type Approach and the Complete Thought Technique is not limited to monologues. Monologues are the foundation; the work that allows you to claim ownership of and showcase your talent. Once mastered, it's time to apply your Castable Types and the Complete Thought Technique to scenes, cold readings and commercial copy as encountered in audition situations.

CHAPTER 5

YOUR CASTABLE TYPES IN ACTION

An audition is a presentation, a pitch meeting, where you demonstrate your talent, professionalism, personality and intelligence as the best fit for the job. You do that by giving a performance. Not a tentative, stumbling, middle of the road reading but a performance. Anything less just won't cut it with so many others making pitches, too.

Giving a performance may seem like an impossible task if you freeze up in auditions or believe the process limits your ability to go all out. That thinking is totally off-base. The very idea provides an easy excuse to cop out at auditions and blame the process for your lack of career success rather than your lack of effective, professional training and focused, savvy effort.

This mind set that accompanies so many actors to auditions comes from the notion that every reading is an unpassable test and the casting associate or talent agent won't like you, won't think you are attractive enough or you will have no clue what to do once you are in the audition room. All of which is utter nonsense. Every auditioner wants you to be at your best. Casting directors would prefer to struggle with the choice of which talented actor to book for the role than watch actors struggle through readings.

Treating every audition as an opportunity to perform your best work and following through by giving an actual performance is the best way to blow the competition out of the water. You will make your presence and talent, through your Castable Types, known to the auditioner, who most assuredly spends too much time watching mediocrity and panic acting.

When you have an audience waiting to be wowed, waiting to find and hire great talent, you have permission to go all out. You *need* to go all out! It's a chance to show how well your Castable Types relate to the camera or audience and bring the script fully to life. Using your Castable Type Monologues is the best way to do this. Your Castable Type Monologue work is completely transferable to every audition format, even when you have to improvise, read sides or cold copy. In fact, the *colder* the audition material, the greater advantage you have using the Castable Types Approach over other actors who panic act their way through the call. You can easily rise above fifty percent of the actors reading for the same role.

USING YOUR CASTABLE TYPES AT AUDITIONS

The research and development you invested in defining your Castable Types through Performance Level monologue work is about to pay dividends. The life contained within each monologue can now be transferred to roles you read for at auditions. Instead of you doing the audition read, let your chosen Castable Type, as realized through your monologue work, do the auditioning for you. This brings a life, specificity and nuance at a Performance Level to your reading

To do this consistently and well, start by organizing your research and development work so it becomes an easy to use support tool.

CREATING A CASTABLE TYPES GUIDEBOOK

Once a library of monologues for each of your Castable Types is assembled, you can begin building your personal guidebook. This will be your source for making smart, insightful choices when building a role and staying on point at auditions and callbacks.

Your guidebook is a tool for keeping you focused and deeply connected to your work. The goal is to get you out of your head and away from the habit of juggling lots of information that becomes an intellectual clog in the flow of emotion and full relaxation. It's a tool to avoid panic acting as it reminds you of all the elements of your Castable Type work so you can make use of it in any audition situation.

The first items to go into your handbook will be copies of your monologues and any research you've done on the writers. Worksheets to help you organize your monologues and create your career plan of action can be downloaded for free from my website, www.independentactor.com. These include forms to help you delineate the Complete Thoughts, Complete Thought Phrases and emotional transitions in each monologue and record the tactile elements and sensorial reactions in your Prior Moments. This will help you assemble the basic materials needed to audition effectively.

The next essential element for keeping your focus at auditions and strengthening your performance is the Concept Board. These bring the visual elements of your monologues, including your look for that particular Castable Type, to life.

Concept Boards

When a costume or set designer is hired to bring a production concept to life, he or she will create sketches and designs along with samples of fabrics, finishes and items that make up the space or outfit and put them all together on a board. These give the creative team a visual and tactile point of reference for what the production will look like on stage or screen. This highly effective tool is a great addition to your guidebook when used to bring your monologue concept to life.

When you first read the script that contained your monologue, images popped into your head, everything from the setting of the scene and what your character looks like to objects or furnishings in the space. A collage of sensory and physical information stayed in your consciousness as you read the story. Now, as you prepare to audition, you will use the Concept Board as a way to bring all that back into your work at a moment's notice.

Search the internet, magazines, catalogues and thrift stores for the materials you need. Get as detailed and crafty as you like using what stimulates your creativity the most for each Concept Board. Find images of what the setting, furniture and outdoor scene looks like or sketch your own. Photo sharing and shopping sites are great for sourcing pictures for this use. Do the same with your character's physical appearance. You can go to a thrift shop and take a few photos of yourself trying on a potential costume item. There may be one part of the look, the fabric of a piece of clothing, for instance, of which you can attach a small swatch to your board. If you've never been to a fabric store, go. You can get one inch swatches of fabric for free on request. Being able actually to feel material can bring your character's physical world instantly to life. Sometimes even a small item, easily taped to your board, can have real meaning. I've used religious medals, baby booties and a puppy collar in the past. One of my coaching clients took a photo of the steering wheel and dashboard from behind the wheel of a pickup truck to trigger the feeling of driving it down a country road, which was part of his Prior Moment work for a monologue. Whatever you choose to include, a simple 8.5 x 11 piece of card stock, which can be purchased for a few cents at a copy shop will make a solid base. Attach your collage of images, swatches, fragments to the card sheet and slip it into a clear page protector for insertion in your guidebook.

I often get eye rolls from my clients when I ask them to create a Concept Board for each monologue, but I always insist it get done. Everyone comes back saying how much fun they had putting it together once they started and how much it added to the depth of creativity in their work, especially with Prior Moments and Layering. For an exercise that takes so little time, it does give a big return. Sitting in the waiting area before an audition is not the time or place to be racking your brain for the visual components of your Castable Type work when you can have them in hand, supporting you instead.

Once you've gathered these first materials to start your guidebook, start putting them together in a slim binder or presentation book solely for this purpose. Don't use anything bulky or unwieldy that is bother to carry with you to auditions.

The guidebook I use personally is a half inch thick, three ring binder with about two dozen pages of material inside of clear page protectors. It's lightweight, does the job and fits easily into my tote bag. Like me, I know you will come to rely on this simple, effective tool to help you follow your audition plan of action.

YOUR AUDITION PLAN OF ACTION

When most actors get to an audition, they follow a predictable routine. Sign in, grab the sides, sit in a chair and try to memorize lines while fighting back nerves for the next five to ten minutes. Not you. You have a plan of action because you have Castable Type work to rely on and it's all laid out in your guidebook. Even for cold readings. Even with only ten minutes to prepare. Your plan is to:

1. Determine which of your Castable Types to use in the audition
2. Choose which of the corresponding monologues to use in full or overlay on to the audition sides or copy
3. Connect your Castable Type character to your audition character
4. Apply the Complete Thought Technique to the sides or copy to breakdown and own the script.
5. Audition confidently at a Performance Level

DETERMINING WHICH CASTABLE TYPE TO USE IN COLD READINGS

Once you have an audition appointment, you'll need to make a few decisions. The first is to determine which of your Castable Types to use. If you self-submitted for the role, then you know what the auditioner saw in your headshot and resume and should have read a breakdown for the character. If your rep secured the audition slot, the breakdown is usually made available to you along with any sides. In either case, you have the information you need to choose which of your Castable Types is the right one to bring to the role. If you don't know much about the part before you arrive at the audition, make a choice based on any information you can glean upon arrival, like seeing the sides or gauging the energy and types of others waiting to go in and read. You may even decide to bring elements of two of your Types to the reading. The simple act of making a decision, making smart choices about the work you are going to present, puts you in charge of your talent and begins building an edge over at least half of the other actors vying for the job.

CHOOSING A CORRESPONDING MONOLOGUE

Your next set of decisions derive from a Clean Reading of the sides or commercial copy you will be using in the audition. Remember to make choices based on the feelings that result from the contextually honest information you get from a start to finish read. This is most important when looking at commercial copy which can be very fragmentary and nonlinear. Stay with your Clean Reading reactions as they should be free of nerve induced projections and anticipated reactions. Once you have the contextual information about who the character is, what his or her wants are, ask yourself these additional questions:

Is this material similar in style or tone to the work of other writers, shows or commercials?

What are the similarities between my Castable Types and the character I will be reading?

Using the answers to these last two questions with the information from your Clean Reading, you will be able to pick the best Castable Type to transfer to the role. You may recognize a writing style, character or just one or two elements of your Castable Types in the sides or copy. Even if it's just an element or two, go with that corresponding monologue character as your working base. If this seems risky to you, remember that you were given an audition slot because you have qualities that relate to the role. Your Castable Types

monologues are the vehicle you use to bring those qualities to the fore and relate them to the auditioner. Making no
choices or relying only on the words on the page of your
sides or copy will not give you what is needed to showcase
your talent and bring the role you are reading to life in the
audition. Don't doubt your Castable Types, use them to be
more present and alive in the audition. The process of Clean
Reading and making a Castable Type choice should take no
more than two minutes.

CONNECTING YOUR CASTABLE TYPE CHARACTER TO THE AUDITION CHARACTER

Using your guidebook, look through your worksheets on
the monologue characters you have mastered. Notes from the
Written Profiles, especially regarding character breakdown
and throughline, will be your area to find connections. Once
you find the strongest, most appropriate connection, you will
know which character to transfer to the reading and begin
your preparation. The crucial part of deconstructing sides
and connecting quickly in auditions is to let the Castable
Type character you are choosing to use transfer to the role
you are now reading.

THE POWER OF PRIOR MOMENTS

As you sit in the waiting room, bring the physical elements of the appropriate Prior Moment alive in your body.
Again, you have your notes and worksheets as well as the
Concept Board created for this piece right in your guidebook.
You will not look out of place if you pull out a slim binder
and look through a few pages while waiting. This is your
only opportunity to focus and prepare so you shouldn't be
doing anything else. This is the job of a professional actor.
Checking your messages or making small talk is not.

Concentrate on the strongest element of your Prior Moment. Look at the Concept Board to focus your attention on
an image, object or texture that will spur you if necessary and
close your eyes for a moment and allow the physical sensation

to come to life. It may be a smell, taste or sensation in one or more parts of your body as it reacts to the feeling of an object or the temperature, for instance. Remember to stay with the physical and not force an anticipated emotional state. Allow your body, not your head, to connect you to the emotions by breathing deeply and naturally. This should take no more than a minute. Once you have this connection active and flowing, turn your attention back to your script.

APPLY THE COMPLETE THOUGHT TECHNIQUE

Actors come across all manner of scripts at auditions. Some sides provided at cold readings are spare and barely fill the page, some are meaty portions from the script or even a complete scene. Commercial copy runs the gamut from one part in a two or multi-person scene to spokesperson style copy to a description of a scene to be improvised. In those instances, you may encounter lines that are nonlinear and imagistic. In my work as a professional coach, I am presented with fresh sides and copy every week that I must help my clients deconstruct and prepare for auditions, usually in a very short amount of time, with minimal background information provided. In all of these situations, Complete Thoughts can be found and used to advantage. This technique helps clarify the throughline, find pace and define the emotional transitions, even in high pressure audition situations, exactly what an auditioner looks for an actor to accomplish at a casting call. My clients rely on me to get the script right and find additional insight that allows their performance to shine and get them to callbacks or book the job outright. I always do by using this approach and you can, too.

First, define the Complete Thoughts and give each a two to three word Complete Thought phrase. Do not fall into the trap of believing a thought has been expressed because another char-acter speaks. The research and development you put into your Castable Types monologues is the majority of the work you will do in any audition. It is really that character, in context, speaking and living the lines. Create *lines between the lines* to connect fragmentary and imagistic copy into a Complete Thought.

Consider the Prior Moment and throughline you are transferring from your Castable Type monologue and compare it to what exists in the sides. Overlay the deep background and emotional work from your Castable Type monologue, making those few adjustments that may be required by audition material. In most cases, you can simply transfer your chosen monologue by thinking and living the monologue while substituting the words of the sides or copy. This works almost every time.

Look at a scene as two inner monologues rather than one conversation. This prevents you from playing into the other character's throughline and losing your own. Focus only on what your character is saying. The crucial part of deconstructing a scene quickly in audition situations is to let the Castable Type character you are transferring do the reading and define the thoughts and not fall into the trap of believing a thought is expressed because another character speaks. The research and development you put into your Castable Types monologues is the majority of the work you will do in any audition. It is really *that* character speaking and living the lines. It is your Castable Type monologue character who is auditioning, not you, trying to pull a disconnected reading out of thin air. Create "lines between the lines" of the dialogue to fill in and define emotional transitions as though the part you are about to read was a monologue, rather than one half of a scene. Keep in mind that, in scenes, two characters will not necessarily come to emotional transitions at the same time. That's fine as it creates comedic or dramatic friction to propel the storyline. So stay, confidently, in your own work.

Next, say the lines on the supporting breath. Keep going with the lines until you feel that a thought has been completely expressed. Then, breathing in again, start the new thought that follows. If the completeness of the thought feels right, make a quick note in pencil of your Complete Thought phrase and underline the key words. If you are reading a two page sitcom script it may take you three minutes to go through this process.

TAKING IT TO PERFORMANCE LEVEL

Now, look over your sides as a dialogue, a scene. Note where your pencil marks are delineating Complete Thoughts and key words and look over your lines between the lines. If you need to adjust the Complete Thought phrases from the transferred monologue, do so now. Then, breathing in, start running the script as though you were doing it with the other character in the scene. Stay with your work but allow yourself to hear the other character's lines and react to them at the same time but staying with your throughline and breathing. Repeat this process until it starts to imprint in your instrument. Remember, you are transferring most of the work you are using to bring this piece to life with adjustments for context and specific details. Let your Castable Type monologue character do the heavy lifting.

Ideally you should be running these lines out loud pre-audition. It is a major mistake to be saying them over and over in your head or quietly under your breath. Those lines never sound the same way or have same depth and energy when said aloud. Now that you understand the connection between breathing and emotion, you should realize that whispering or speaking silently cuts that off. In a waiting room setting you do not want to be disruptive but it is an audition. You should be actively preparing to show your work. Find a corner and say your lines to the wall or facing a window if it makes you feel better. The more you do this the less self-conscious you will become. Professionals prepare. Amateurs get embarrassed, self-conscious and psyched out when they see the pros at work. Use this to your advantage!

Keep place and Prior Moment vibrant. Let these layers inform your pace and give texture to your work. Stay connected to your supporting breath as that is imprinting the thoughts within you and energizing your physical life. As you get more confident with each run through of your sides, allow more of your nuanced behavior to come in to the work at the emotional transitions.

If we go with an average waiting time of ten minutes, you will have a full four to five minutes to be running your sides. For material used in cold readings, this is plenty of time. If you get sides in advance, more time can be devoted to the process. If you have the opportunity to perform one of your monologues, use your waiting room time to review the materials in your guidebook as you connect to your already prepared work.

INSIDE THE AUDITION ROOM

Once you enter the audition room, you should be given your mark or a place to stand and any instructions the auditioner may want you to follow. It's at this point that you should ask any intelligent questions you may have regarding the material or the audition procedure. That could include getting the correct pronunciation of a word or name, clarifying plot points or the relationship between characters or getting the level of humor or physicality. Keep in mind that a casting director wants you to have all the information you need to feel relaxed and do your best work.

As you take your mark, look around the space you have to work in and lay in elements of your place on to it. You may have to stay on your mark if the audition is recorded but that doesn't mean you are in a bubble. Think about how we converse with people. We may be standing or sitting in one place for a few minutes while talking back and forth. That doesn't mean we are static and unaffected by the surroundings. Standing in a bedroom doorway looking at a sleeping child, on line to check out or in front of a merchandise display at a store are perfect examples of being active in and affected by place. Let this bring context and authenticity to your audition.

Once on your mark and after slating (if asked to do so), take in a few supporting breaths. Use these to reconnect to your Prior Moment, Complete Thought Phrase and key words and then begin your audition. If you keep your Castable Type monologue character fully involved and allow him or her to live the moments of your audition material you will be giving a more in-depth performance than the majority of the actors vying for the role. If you keep connected to the Complete Thoughts and energize them with breath, your work will be at the top of the short list.

On Camera vs. Live

There is a deeply entrenched myth that acting on camera is subtle and small while on stage it is big and broad. This is one of the most foolish ideas out there. I could cite myriad examples of delicate, filmic stage work and big, broad films just from the last few seasons. Rather than wasting pages demolishing this fallacy, realize that the key to doing a great audition in front of the camera or in front of an audience is being fully alive in the role, completely connected to the throughline and relating all this to the camera or audience. That's what you should be doing already if you are using this technique.

You won't be moving or speaking any differently. You will be adjusting your focus. For on-camera auditions you either use the camera as your point of focus (as in the person you are relating to) or a reader. If you are working with a reader use him or her as you would another actor. Just don't expect much reaction. Readers do not give full performances as a rule so the work of the actor auditioning can be the sole focus. If you are auditioning for an agent or theatre, put your focus immediately to the side of the person watching you at eye level. Never look the person in the eye. That takes the individual out of the role of audience member and makes him or her your scene partner. Auditioners want to be in the audience. An agent or casting director can't evaluate your work if they are in the scene with you. Never make your focus the ceiling, over the person's head or off to one side for more than a moment. When you do that for more than a second or two, the energy of your performance is lost to the rafters or wings.

Adjustments

It's impossible to predict exactly what you may be asked to do in audition situations,

But here are a few givens.

Actors are often asked to make changes in the work they are presenting, which are called adjustments. These may be as simple as asking you to pick up or slow down the pace or make a slight change in the tone of your reading. An adjustment is not a criticism of your talent or your worth as an actor. It's just an adjustment, a way to bring you closer to what the auditioner believes will be needed when in production. There is no way for any actor to know exactly how the director will want the role to be realized at the time of audition so adjustments are gifts to help your work better suit the project. The ability to make adjustments quickly and thoroughly is a big boost to your castability. Scripts are often incomplete at the time of casting and directors want the ability to make creative changes. An actor who can't make adjustments is like a great big boulder in the middle of the set. Everyone has to work around it. Don't be that rock.

Process adjustments through your Castable Type character. That is the person auditioning so changes filter through him or her. Don't rush into the work once given an adjustment. It's not only self-defeating to your performance, it looks like you aren't taking the time to think about what you have just been asked to change. Take a moment or two to integrate the new information or situation and then begin your work.

IMPROVISATIONAL AUDITIONS

Improvisational ability is one of the most in-demand tools an actor can possess. When asked to improvise in audition situations, think of this as an opportunity to show more of your Castable Type character. Since you've researched and developed this character in depth, you have a wealth of background and history from which to draw. In all improvisation, stakes, urgency and reaction are the keys. Never fall into the trap of explaining what your reaction or stakes are, show them and take your time to do it

DIALOGUE-FREE AUDITIONS

I deal with these most in commercial auditions. An example was a car commercial I auditioned for a few years ago. Rather than sides, a description of the commercial action was provided. As a passenger in the car on a trip through a scenic stretch of road, I was to take in and be moved by the beauty of the surroundings and the fact that I was sharing the experience with friends who were with me on the drive. Once the casting associate hit record on the camera all I had to do was allow my Castable Type character to experience the beauty of the sights seen through the passenger window.

If you're in a dialogue-free audition, use emotional transitions to take you from connection to connection, reaction to reaction. Don't indicate what you are experiencing, just live each moment fully and completely allowing your nuanced behaviors to do the talking for you.

REACTION SHOTS

Some auditions are little more than slating and giving a reaction. Slating, if you are new to the business, is saying your name and representation information on camera so decision makers know whom they are watching and how to get in contact with that actor during playback. Slates should always be given in your own voice, as yourself. Do not slate in character. Slate simply, clearly and with a natural smile. This is you talking. Let anyone who sees your slate know that you are a friendly, normal, professional who will be a pleasure to have on the set. Slating is often your only chance to show that fact.

Reaction shots come in many forms. You may be asked innocuous questions about the weather or your favorite song just to get the way you look when thinking and speaking on camera. You may be asked to react to something specific like the aroma or taste of delicious food, opening a gift or watching a movie. Unless instructed otherwise, treat these like improvised auditions and take your time experiencing every aspect of what you are reacting to in a natural and authentic manner. Slowing down your reactions allows the nuance to shine through.

WRAPPING YOUR AUDITION

Once your audition is completed, a simple "thank you" is all you need to say or should expect. Unless you are performing in an appointment for possible representation, you should not expect critique on your work or an evaluation of your talent. Casting is a time sensitive process. Pick up your bag and get out or risk ruining the good impression your work has just made by coming across as a needy, desperate actor.

Once you've exited the audition studio, make a few quick notes on your work in your guidebook regarding how you put your Castable Type to use and the type of material you read. This information will help you further refine your types and the way the industry sees you.

CHAPTER 6

GETTING THE PERFECT CASTABLE TYPE HEADSHOT

You know the look. The one of surprise on the face of the casting director as you walk through the audition room door. The casting director stares right through you, waiting for the actor in the headshot to appear. That's because the actor in your headshot bears only faint resemblance to the one that made it to the audition. You've now punked the only person in the room who could hire you for a paying gig and set yourself up as a time wasting fool. In the previous chapters of this book you learned about your Castable Types and how to bring that specific and unique energy to your auditions and performances. Now it's time to bring your Castable Types to your marketing materials and create a complete, professional package selling your talent to the industry.

HEADSHOTS: THE BOTTOM LINE

Headshots must look like you and project your Castable Types. If they don't accomplish that singular purpose, they're working against you and should never be used for submissions. Period. One of the biggest mistakes made by actors is to go automatically for a pretty or edgy model-like look, rather than one that exemplifies their Castable Types. Casting directors expect to see exactly the same person in the photo walk through their door for an audition. That's the person they called in for a reading, that's whom they wish to see. If someone else shows up, a completely different Castable Type, an audition slot will have been wasted and the casting director will not be happy. Don't make this mistake! If your headshots are an inaccurate depiction of the types of characters you play well, then your headshots can't be trusted and casting offices will pick up on this in no time and know to avoid you in the future.

The same is true for outdated shots. You may not have changed much in the last five years but styles certainly have. If the shot itself appears dated, the assumption will be that it must be an inaccurate picture of you and you aren't professional enough to keep your most basic and important marketing tool up to date. If you're usually called in for geeky roles, don't waste money producing a sexy, upscale photo. If you get cast as a geek as well as a sexy, romantic type then devote equal time and energy to capturing each Castable Type fully and completely and use your pictures accordingly.

Examples from a Castable Types Headshot Shoot

photo by: IAP

Different Castable Types require their own marketing materials. Don't try to cut corners by using one, middle of the road, general shot. The look used and personality projected in your headshot must be a look you can recreate and a personality that comes through at auditions and interviews. If this isn't the case then you've wasted your time and money, no matter how great the photo or how much the photographer and your friends like the shots. Trying to get by or make do with headshots that are inaccurate - using them because you paid for them - is a very bad decision. If your core marketing is just plain bad, the results will be, too.

WHEN TO GET NEW HEADSHOTS

You should have your pictures taken as often as the

development of your Castable Types dictate or changes to your look and current styles require, not simply because the calendar has changed. Think of each photo session as adding pictures to your library of headshots as opposed to replacing what you've been using. Prune truly outdated shots that no longer represent your types as necessary.

Unless there's a significant change in hairstyle, weight, or cosmetic improvements, well done Castable Type headshots can work for one to two years at the maximum. You may want to expand upon one of your types with another quick shoot if it becomes a hot type for you and brings in more bookings and interest.

Child and teen actors *must* have annual updates as they're constantly changing and maturing. They should stay away from clichéd, age-specific shots such as askew baseball caps, peeking over adult sized sunglasses perched halfway down the nose, or sports shots. Young actors have unique, interesting and highly marketable Castable Types and shouldn't be pushed into stereotyped poses. Those headshots scream "stage mom on board" and can really backfire by scaring off agents. If acting is truly a fun activity your child enjoys, allow him or her the chance to work with a stylist and define the look for the kind of roles they have booked or been called in to read. Most stylists are happy to work with a well-mannered child or teen if they have well-mannered parents who allow the stylist to do his or her craft.

If you're an older actor, don't be afraid to flaunt your age. Mature actors who look their age, whether in a healthy, fit and active way or in a way that shows the sins of the past, are always in demand. The talent pool gets smaller as people get older and leave the industry. It isn't uncommon for actors to book far more consistently later in their career so don't fall prey to the notion that you must look as young as possible. Don't be afraid to smile if it shows a few wrinkles around your eyes. Just stay true to your Castable Types, look your authentic best and don't shy away from showing more of your body in headshots.

THE KEY TO GETTING THE PERFECT CASTABLE TYPE HEADSHOT

When you hire a headshot photographer, you're employing an independent contractor to do a job for your business, namely capturing your Castable Types on film in the most striking way possible. Most headshot photographers have a set pattern to which they adhere in an effort to run shoots efficiently and profitably achieving what they consider professional results. While that's perfectly understandable from the photographer's point of view, it's rarely in the best interest of the actor paying for the session. That pattern becomes the photographer's signature, their look, their style of taking headshots. More often than not it produces photos that speak only of the person who took them and say nothing about the person in them. The more established a headshot photographer becomes the more entrenched their signature style. Angles, lighting, backgrounds and set up of the shots become immediately recognizable as the work of particular photographers. Casting directors see many thousands of headshots in a season and can actually spot the work of many photographers with just a cursory glance. I've held seminars with casting directors who have done just that and listened while they told actors what I have just told you: they wouldn't have called them in because they knew their headshot was selling the photographer and not the actor, they didn't trust what they saw in the picture and didn't have time to waste auditioning people who are wrong for the part.

Obviously, headshot photographers would argue this point. They'll show you their portfolios filled with dozens of actors of all different types as a testament to their personalized service and dedication to capturing the individual on film. But what good does it do you to look at a book full of strangers? How would you know if their Castable Types were jumping off the page or if the photo truly resembled the actor? The obligatory shots of famous television and movie actors are no help either. Everyone knows what their Castable Type and look is and actors who have established themselves or have some degree of fame usually go for a more general, relaxed shot so as not to be overly identified with one project or role.

You don't.

Once you have defined your Castable Types and brought them to life through monologue work in tandem with a top coach or by using this book as a guide, you find a great stylist who will help you refine the looks of your Castable Types in a way that is current for your target markets. Someone who, together with your input, will show you how to achieve the look of your Castable Types while appearing authentic and natural, during your photo shoot and at auditions and on-camera readings as well. With the services of a professional stylist the balance of artistic expression shifts back to you and insures that the look you need to project is readily available to be photographed. Then you may easily choose a technically proficient photographer. You can discern this from browsing through portfolios and rating prowess with lighting, backgrounds and shot set up. Then consider price, scheduling and re-shoot policy to narrow your search and make a final selection.

Do beware! Some photographers will try to sell you on their ability to style, apply makeup, and arrange hair. They'll tell you that no one else understands the way they use lighting or that it's better to have a distraction-free session. Some photographers will tell you they'll only work with a particular stylist and don't allow others into the studio because they may be bothersome, unprofessional, or in the way. Run from these photographers as fast as you can: they only want to do things their way and will not take your needs into account, to any degree or for any price.

Truly professional photographers, the ones who work on cover art, lifestyle spreads and get hired for celebrity portraiture, are accustomed to working with teams of stylists and creative directors, many of whom they meet for the first time as the shoot begins. Professionals can adapt. It's

113

perfectly natural for photographers to have a favored stylist with whom they like to partner and whom you may well want to consider using. The ugly truth, however, is that the favorite "stylist" of many a headshot photographer is often a pal, significant other or an aspiring model working as an assistant in exchange for a free portfolio. These geniuses figure they've learned enough by osmosis to keep the shine off the face of some struggling actor. Once you've seen the amazing difference a professionally trained stylist can make, you'll forever understand why they're the key component in achieving great results with your photos. You'll never again allow untrained hands to have a say in your headshots.

If you've worked in film or television, you've likely encountered professional makeup artists with whom you may want to work. If not, get referrals from actors who have worked recently or peruse the myriad websites featuring stylist portfolios and resumes. If you're located outside of New York or Los Angeles, you'll find professional, camera savvy makeup artists working at your local television stations, more than likely on a news program. You can also find styling pros through their labor union, which is a local of the International Alliance of Theatrical Stage Employees (IATSE), the Professional Beauty Network (www.professionalbeauty.net) Stage 32 (www.stage32.com) or The Make-up Artist Network (www.makeupartistnetwork.com), or the latter two being online resource directories of make-up artists. Remember that makeup artists travel to shoots on location all year long. The person you want to work with could be in your corner of the world on a project so never feel out of the loop.

Working With a Professional Stylist

The next step is to book consultations with the two or three stylists you are considering. Explain in depth the Castable Types you want to evoke in your photo shoot and at auditions. Although you may pay, on average $50.00 to $100.00 for a one hour consult, you're investing in the development and presentation of your most marketable self for your photo shoot and auditions. This is just a fraction of the cost of headshots, but will guarantee far better pictures and a look that you can use confidently in auditions. The start of a headshot shoot isn't the best moment to meet your stylist for the first time and the 30 minutes or so allotted to the preparation of your look isn't enough time to get on the same page and truly bring out the best visual aspects of your Castable Types. A photographer will not take a dozen shots to see if you like the results, but a stylist will do your hair and makeup in a paid consult and give you jpeg pictures to take home so you can see the results and make informed choices and changes. Rushing around, feeling pressured into the suggestions of a makeup artist you don't know and a photographer trying to stick to a schedule will only turn you into a nervous wreck in front of the camera with lousy headshots as a result. Don't be pennywise and pound foolish with your most important marketing and publicity tool.

Getting it Right: Before and After the Castable Types Approach to headshots.

photo by: Interface

photo by: IAP

Once you've booked a stylist, discuss the amount of time and money you can spend on the continuing upkeep of your look. Don't get talked into a really short haircut, extensions or multi-layered highlights for your headshots if you don't have the time, money, or patience to keep the look up for the year(s) in which you use those photos. Don't do an ultra-natural look if you always wear makeup or have a very hip or sophisticated hairstyle. Great stylists will not only have the talent to help define the look of your Castable Type and

115

teach you how to maintain it; they'll also have solutions to skin and hair issues. Most will work with your reasonable budget because headshot shoots are straightforward and normally take just about an hour to complete. Employing a stylist is much like employing a private acting coach: these are professionals, totally focused on taking *your look* a step up the ladder to a performance level, with all the edges polished and exuding confidence.

Ensuring A Successful Photo Shoot

When meeting with a photographer, you should apprise him or her of the two or three Castable Types you want to capture and how much of your body you would like to include in the shot; three-quarters, waist up, head and shoulders, standing, or sitting. The photographer should also know how many shots you want to devote to capturing a particular Castable Type and how many clothing, hair or makeup changes you require.

This approach is a seismic shift in the way most actors handle headshots. The old way of turning over your most important marketing tool to a total stranger, someone who knows nothing about you as an actor, has no idea – no matter what they may claim—about the casting process and will inevitably rely on their own working style, is utterly ridiculous. It's a surefire formula for wasted money, wasted time and ineffective pictures. You must take charge of your headshots, always keeping in mind that you are hiring people to make your business more successful and to make you and your Castable Types more marketable. With your types determined, well-defined and a working budget in mind, you'll find choosing a photographer easier than ever before. A truly talented photographer will welcome an actor who can articulate what he or she needs to accomplish with headshots. A true professional will have no qualms working with another professional, be it your on-set coach or your stylist.

Wardrobe and Grooming

What you wear in your photos is what you should wear

to auditions. These are your Castable Type looks and should be part of a consistent marketing plan. Wear nothing in your headshots that would be uncomfortable, cumbersome or unflattering to wear in an audition. If you purchase new clothing for the shoot ask yourself if you would really wear it to a casting call. If not, leave it on the rack. Most of the time, the building blocks of a wardrobe that suits your Castable Types are already hanging in your closet. Build on what you've got, replacing worn, dated or ill-fitting items as necessary then buy the items that are missing.

Today's headshots are done in color. When choosing your wardrobe, think of your color story as complimenting your individual skin and hair tones and your Castable Types energy. Wear solid color items with clean, well fitted lines. The industry wants to see your body line and shape, no matter what it may be, not the work of a clothing designer. Layers can add subtle visual interest and complimentary lines as long as they don't add bulk. Forget the accessories and the jewelry. Neither belongs in your headshot. With the exception of a belt, if the garment doesn't work on its own, don't wear it. Stay away from oversized collars and cowl necks, busy prints, checks, stripes and blocks of white or very pale colors that will read as pure white or overwhelming colors that take the focus off of you and put it on the garment. The color black should also be used sparingly and never with younger actors as it looks too sophisticated. Black absorbs light and can look flat and dead on camera unless very carefully lit. If you don't want your headshot to look like a floating head in a sea of flatness, wear black sparingly. Jewel tones, earth tones and soft pastels are usually good choices, dependent on your personal skin and hair tone.

Keep in mind that your eyes and your mouth are the focal points of your facial expression. Be sure that both areas are neatly groomed with clean lines for clarity of communication: no uni-brows, crooked goatees, unshaped brows, untrimmed beards, etc. You may also need to do some pruning if you're a really hairy guy and it shows through the neckline of shirts and sweaters. Shave it, thread it, wax it – get rid of it. You should also visit your dentist and have your teeth cleaned and whitened a week or two before your photo session. Keep your bright smile going with an at home or over the counter kit.

Men should consider getting a professional shave the day of your photo shoot. Even if you plan on keeping a little bit of facial hair for some of the shots; you can shave off the rest yourself. This is not the time to have nicked, sensitive, red or bumpy skin. A professional shave will leave your skin in a healthy, well hydrated state and give you a chance to relax before your shoot.

Prominently featuring tattoos or exposing lots of bare skin is a great way to take away from the Castable Type you should be showcasing. The more of the former, the less of the later we actually notice. This is a pet peeve of every casting director I know. If you are seriously inked, that can become a type unto itself. You should have shots selling that side of you that but don't limit your acting range to your tats. Also, most casting directors prefer that hands stay away from the face in headshots.

BACKGROUND AND LIGHTING

Keep the backgrounds of your headshots simple. Think tonal or textural. Don't compete with plants, staircases, windows or shadows. The photo should be focused solely on you. Remember that these shots are for marketing purposes; they are not about formal or art photography. They're supposed to sell *you* not the photographer. Choose solid backgrounds in shades that enhance your coloring. If you're very fair or very dark skinned a black backdrop will make you look like a floating head or completely swallow you up. Shades of gray in a light to medium range are always worth trying as they work well with almost everyone. The most modern look is an all-white background created with a professional paper roll. Keep both your skin and hair color in mind when choosing as the backdrop should complement you and never be too close or contrasting in color.

You'll never act in purely natural light so never have your headshots taken that way. If a photographer tells you that he or she only uses natural light or wants to shoot outdoors, leave. You need to present yourself as you would look if hired and that will almost always be with artificial, managed and reflected light. Even on indie films or outdoor stages there is a mix of lighting sources in use and you should sell yourself in the same visual milieu in which you plan to be working.

You also need to look your castable best and that requires a managed studio background and theatrical makeup for men and women regardless of whether or not you wear makeup on a regular basis. Studio lighting and flash photography create shadows, highlights and lowlights. No one ever looks the same in still photography as they do in person. That's why you need professional eyes to counter the shadows and shine, soften or sharpen angles and keep you looking like you. That's why women and men need studio lighting and professional makeup.

MAINTAINING YOUR FOCUS DURING THE PHOTO SHOOT

The purpose of your headshots is to market you, your energy, types and talent. This comes through your eyes, facial expression and body language. You must always elicit your Castable Types from the inside as well as the outside. Don't just sit there and listen to music or chat away between the flash. Be in the prior moments of the appropriate Castable Type monologues so that you are truly, deeply and honestly projecting the life of the character. Be in their world, not yours or the photographer's. Your headshot must say something; speak for you when you aren't there to do it in person, essentially auditioning for you before you ever get a call. Make sure it does the job.

*A great set of CastableType shots for an
Actor's Comp Card for Commerical/Print Work*

photo by: TAP

CHOOSING THE RIGHT PHOTOS

When reviewing your photos and choosing which shots to reproduce, don't solicit the opinion of the photographer, family, or friends. You want to make choices with the eye of a casting director and your Castable Types in mind. You should be able to make informed choices and if you can't decide between shots enlist the help of someone who understands your thinking process and ultimate goal, like a trusted professional coach. Ignore the choices of your photographer; you must clearly view every shot with no influence other than an eye toward capturing your Castable Types.

Reproductions of your headshots should always have a border of some size as they're heavily handled. Have your professional name printed on the front in the border. Don't print any other information, such as phone number, union affiliation or an e-mail address on the front of your picture; it doesn't belong there and detracts from the purpose and impact of the headshot.

ACTORS COMP CARDS

Casting Directors need believable people of all ages, shapes and sizes to appear in print and on-camera advertising. Submitting a single headshot locks you in to one look and type, limiting your chances of booking a breakthrough job in commercials.

Actors Composite (or Comp) Cards are highly effective tools for increasing the odds of booking commercial work and making a powerful impression with agents and managers. Comp Cards give you a visual way to showcase your range of Castable Types in a simple 5 x 8 format. Using four to six shots - a single shot on one side of the card and four to five shots on the other side of the card, you can show more of the expressions, reactions, body and physical life you relate well. Comp Card shots can be taken in a range of settings outside the studio with natural light. The idea is to give a mix of images that look like they could be production stills, print work and publicity shots. You can use those big personality photos that pop off the screen with confidence on a comp card.

LOVING YOUR HEADSHOTS

Your headshots are an end product of developing your Castable Types. If you've embraced who you are from a casting point of view, capturing that person on film is a much easier job than trying to conform to the expected look of a stunningly attractive leading actor or clownish sidekick second banana. It's about showing your individual talent to the people who can help you book work. Your photo shoot shouldn't feel like an onerous, depressing, stress-inducing chore but a creative outlet for the roles your talent and personality embody. Think about your shoot as though it's a performance where, for once, you have total artistic control. You've hired a team to put the production elements in place and now it's up to you to enjoy the opportunity to act out what you do best as an actor.

Plan your headshot shoot for a time when you are completely in charge of your Castable Types, have taken the time to work with a stylist on developing the look, comfortably chosen the wardrobe, are rested and healthy and have selected a photographer who will work with your professional needs and budget. Then relax and enjoy your time in front of the camera. Great results will follow!

CHAPTER 7

MARKETING MATERIALS: BIOS, RESUMES AND MORE

Headshots are the core component of your marketing materials but there are other, equally important items professional actors must have to effectively sell their talent.

RESUMES THAT WORK FOR YOU

Resumes are a focused synopsis of your credits and training. That synopsis should guide the reader to the markets and types that you would most successfully book. A resume should never include everything you've done, only what matters now. Time, success, physical changes, and maturity will tell you what credits to remove and when. Your resume is always a careful balance of the newest, most appropriate and most desirable credits. Updating and editing your resume each season will keep you in touch with the way the industry perceives your Castable Types and the genres in which you are currently having the most success.

The look of your resume needs to reflect your personality, style and Castable Types through its graphic design. Your name, phone number, union affiliations, email and photo at the top should create a logo and should also be used on letterhead, postcards, and insert cards or labels for demo reels. This logo is a way of visually branding your marketing materials with the same quality and energy that you present as an actor. Choose fonts characteristic of your Castable Type for your name and headers. Although the "less is more" rule is usually a reliable guide, don't be afraid to experiment or try something new. Let your natural creativity shine through on paper.

Beneath your logo, the layout should follow a format of three columns on an 8 x 10 page with enough of a border on the sides and bottom so credits are not smudged when the document is handled. Casting departments will write notes on your resume so print it on good quality white or light colored paper and use a glue stick to attach it to your photo. Don't print your resume directly onto the photo backing, it always smudges and if notes are written on it, indentations will appear on your face. Don't use staples as they catch on everything and tear your materials. Don't use fluorescent or primary-colored paper. It isn't eye-catching, just ugly, and if you have your picture on your resume it looks like a clip from the opening credits to *The Partridge Family* and that was hideous—even in the 70's. Your headshot and resume are an advertisement for you—if you wouldn't publish this "ad" in a magazine, don't send it out to the industry.

ORGANIZING YOUR ACTING CREDITS

Credits should be placed in the following categories:
Film
Television
Theatre
Commercials
New Media
Industrials
Voiceovers
Print

Use only the categories in which you have credits. It isn't necessary or expected to have worked in all genres, nor would they all fit on a single resume. If you have sparse credits in related categories, a couple of student films and an under five on a soap for example, combine the two under Film/Television. If you haven't yet made a commercial or voiceover, do not put "conflicts available upon request" under those headings. You aren't fooling anyone and that phrase is actually code for "I've never booked a commercial or voice over in my life."

Your strongest category should be at the top of your resume. If you just moved to Los Angeles and have lots of great theatre credits, keep those at the top. If you're in New York and have mostly commercials and television gigs under your belt, that's what you lead with. Always put your strongest category first, and the best credits within that category at the top. Don't undersell or undercut your good work. Don't follow a chronological order. Don't think that, because you're in New York or Los Angeles, theatre or film must be first. Your best work must be first, always.

Within a category you may find it beneficial to delineate credits further. For instance, you may opt to have your stage credits divided into Off-Broadway and Theatre as opposed to simply Theatre. Television credits might be placed into Starring, Guest Star and Recurring roles. Do this only to accent certain credits that deserve a bit of extra attention, not to take up space on the page. One good reason for using these sub-headings might be that you were in one or two pilots or Off-Broadway plays that had short runs or were at small, emerging theaters and you don't want those credits to blend in with the showcases and readings also in your theatre category. You may have done several one-person shows, national tours or performed at the Edinburgh Festival. These are great reasons to make a separate header with those titles. This way of categorizing may also work in other areas; voiceovers, for instance, might be divided into narration and commercials or national and regional. Again, only make these distinctions to draw attention to multiple credits worth special note. Otherwise it becomes a visual distraction. Make only one or two sub-headings per category.

List acting credits in three columns: project title, role, and production credit. If the role is non-titled or not immediately recognizable, you may put starring, featured, supporting, or cameo in parentheses next to it. This is commonly employed with indie film credits or if your role on a television series was listed as "Man with Briefcase" but was more than a background or extra player. It is rarely used for theatre credits.

Production credits can take a bit more consideration. They need to enhance, specify, or drop the name of someone of note who was involved with the project and still fit into the space allotted for their column. If you were in a play at The Goodman Theater in Chicago, the name itself says it all: a top professional venue housing union productions with an international reputation. If you were in the same play at the Village Playhouse in Skokie, well, that says nothing. So you may opt to use the name of the director or producer as a credit instead. Or, you starred in an undistributed independent film but had a scene with the director's godmother, an Oscar nominated actress. You should certainly list the production credit as "Co-Starring so and so" as opposed to the name of the unknown production company or it's yet to be discovered director.

If you worked with a theatre, production company or director on multiple projects, group them together but alternate the production credits. If that's impossible, use ditto marks. If you did seven plays in a season with one organization, don't list all of them, just your starring roles or the roles that give focus to your Castable Types and the work you would like to be hired for in the future.

If you've appeared in a film or play that was a festival entrant or award winner or you personally won an award for your performance, make a note of that on your resume using an asterisk after the credit title and the name of the award beneath it in a smaller type font. That would also be the credit you would want to appear at the top of your resume.

Any of your performance credits that have an online presence such as a video link or a project website can have the link appear in smaller type underneath the credit.

Training and Special Skills

Two other headers that should appear on your resume are *Training* and *Special Skills.* Training is reserved strictly for your tuition as a performer. You may also add another header, *Education,* if you attended a college or university drama program or if you graduated from a four year school with a degree and feel that it adds to your overall package as a working professional. If you attended vocational school, community or Bible college, leave this category off your acting resume.

Promoting your training credits follows the same basic rules as your acting credits in that you will probably not include all your classes and teachers, just the most important ones. Everyone knows that actors are always in some class or seminar but that doesn't mean that they should all be listed on your resume. The training category is about your core technique and your professional polish, not a list of all the six-session cold reading classes you signed up for so you could meet a sub-agent or the "24 casting directors in 24 weeks" programs. Listing those career school courses can actually backfire on you. The agent or casting director reading your resume may wonder why their colleague, who worked with you in a class, never actually hired you for anything. Leave the crap off, put the core on.

You can break down your training credits using any combination of the headers below which are applicable, or fashion ones better suited to your personal training background:

ACTING
> Acting Technique, Scene Study, Sensory, Method, Meisner, Monologues, Text Breakdown, Camera Technique, Shakespeare, Comedia Del' Arte

SPEECH OR VOICE
> Speech, Diction, Linklater, Skinner, Voice, IPA, Accents, Dialects, Alexander Technique, Cartoon Voices, Singing (Jazz, Gospel, etc.)

MOVEMENT OR DANCE
> Laben, Lecoq, Viewpoints, Suzuki, Feldenkrais, Historical Styles, Tap, Jazz, Modern, Drumming, Interpretive Dance, Tai Chi, Tribal, African, Stage Combat, Fencing, Broad Swords, Stunts, Historical Movement

COMEDY OR STYLES
> Improv, Stand Up, Sketch Comedy, Clowning, Mask, Puppetry, Stunts

These are the basic areas of study for most actors. Classes devoted to cold reading skills, soaps or how to audition don't belong on your resume as they assume you already have mastered an acting technique and are simply honing a particular skill. Obviously, if you have no other acting classes to list then you will have to put those career courses on your resume, but that should serve as a wake-up call: get into a real acting class and learn your craft immediately.

Follow the same three-column format for listing training credits as acting credits: name of class, instructor, and school, studio or private coaching. Some private coaches tell their clients to list an elite studio or university next to their credit since they also teach there or have taught there in the past. This is wrong. If you aren't matriculated at that school or studio and taking instruction on location then you should never claim it as a credit. Just because your coach is a member of the Actors Studio doesn't mean you are too, by virtue of association.

It isn't necessary to repeat information like the name of a school. Simply group those teachers together and use ditto marks in the appropriate column. If you had many acting instructors over the years, list only the three or four that taught your core technique, were the most influential, inspirational, or have the most notable reputation.

The final section, *Special Skills*, is a part of the resume underestimated and underutilized by most actors. Your special skills create an image of how physical, active or agile you are – vitally important when you consider that an audition may consist of little more than you standing in place and slating. You may be a large person but a gifted physical actor and graceful to boot. What you present in this portion of your resume can get that message across to the reader. It's also where you can tout specialty skills that make you particularly castable for certain roles, including being multi-lingual, mastering accents, or playing an instrument.

Begin Special Skills with any languages you speak other than English. Use "Speak" or "Speak Fluently" and then list the individual languages. Do not put "Basic" – if you cannot speak the language passably or fluently there are plenty of other actors who do, and they will be hired, not someone with basic skills.

Then list the accents and dialects you have mastered. Be sure to list only those that suit your Castable Types. Include all the regional and contemporary dialects of your home country that you have studied. For Americans that might include, New England, South Boston, Brooklyn, Mid Atlantic, Midwestern, Southern, Puerto Rican, Caribbean and Standard American Stage. You can get creative with your own colorful, specific, titles such as Urban Girl, West Texas Redneck, and Gangsta Thug. Just be sure the description, dialect and your Castable Type are in sync and that you have truly mastered the accent.

Next, make a list of ten to twelve physical activities that you could portray truthfully and realistically on camera for the duration of a commercial, about thirty seconds. If you can serve a tennis ball and volley for a few minutes then tennis may be one of your special skills. Watch commercials to get an idea of the sport and leisure activities that are featured in ads that suit your Castable Types to help you focus your list. Then add the physical and agility items that you like to do in your everyday life. The point is to paint an active image: "shoot firearms" or "juggling" belong on a resume, computer skills, needlework, photography or crossword puzzles, do not. The same goes for extra listings like owning costumes, uniforms or driving a car. If you are interested in extra work, register online or send your resume to the appropriate agencies with "available for extra work" written on the envelope and at the bottom of your resume and you will probably get a call to go stand somewhere for half a day for a few bucks.

If you play an instrument, have musical, dance or stunt skills that weren't covered in the Training section, this is the place to list them. Finally, add in that special something that you do well and could be an asset to your being cast. I have students who work as dog walkers and preschool teachers so they have, "handle dogs professionally" and "works well with young children" at the end of the skills section. Make use of this area to sell your physically active self. Agencies create databases of clients and freelancers by their special skills so you can use this resume section to open the door to opportunities that you may not have been considered for by virtue of your acting credits alone.

When it comes to your resume, keep it real. Anyone who has worked in this business for any period of time can pick apart a resume filled with lies in the blink of an eye. There is just no good reason to prevaricate. Everyone has to start somewhere, at some time, and agents and casting directors know this. You will not be punished or laughed at for having just a handful of credits. Often, casting directors are looking specifically for fresh faces because that's what an ad agency has requested; a non-union actor with fewer credits because the production company isn't budgeted to pay more than scale. But when an agent reads a phony resume—having starring or featured television credits when you aren't SAG-AFTRA, for instance—why would they want to waste time with you? Now your training and talent become suspect as well. Remember, this is a business: would you submit a resume to a Fortune 500 company filled with lies and think it would never come back to haunt you? Your resume is a marketing tool which you can build season after season. It can't help you grow your business if it doesn't honestly reflect who you are and what you have accomplished. If you are unhappy with your credits or feel that you have been heading in the wrong direction, then make a change. Don't lie.

Bios: Your Secret Weapon

A bio is a complete and polished depiction of you as an actor and a person, a tool which, when used effectively, can develop a deeper interest in you, elicit personal and project publicity and become a deal-closer in interviews.

Most actors think of bios as a brief few lines listing their acting credits in a playbill or press kit but they're really so much more and can be used in a variety of situations. I have all my private students write a bio prior to creating a resume.

This helps them to develop a more fully rounded idea of themselves as artists. Once the bio is completed, it's a simple process to extract credits that truly belong on your current resume and the special skills that should accompany them.

Bios create a total image of you as a castable actor, an industry professional and a well-rounded person. A resume speaks of your accomplishments as a performer and highlights your training while a bio does those things in depth as well as painting a picture of your personal interests and intellect.

Follow a four paragraph format of about five or six sentences each. Write in an active tense but refer to yourself in the third person:

> TRACY ROBERTS MOST RECENTLY APPEARED IN THE FILM *Smear Factor*......

Paragraph 1 mentions your most recent and upcoming roles. Reinforce your Castable Types by defining lesser known projects with images:

> ...*a wicked satire of "gross-out" culture and the reality television craze.*

If your recent projects have all been in a similar vein or veered away from your Castable Types and the direction you would like to pursue, go ahead and add in older credits to keep your image on track and demonstrate range.

Paragraph 2 is where you name-drop, citing any well-known playwrights, producers, directors or actors with whom you have worked. It's also the place to write in more depth regarding your formal education, training and the teachers or scholars of note who shaped your artistry. If you were mentored by a famous director, accepted into a theatre company apprentice program, or nominated for awards, you can spell it all out in paragraph 2.

Paragraph 3 picks up with the rest of your credits, usually the ones that are a bit older or carry less artistic clout, such as television commercials, voiceovers or print work. Of course, if your career focus is voiceovers or commercials then they are the subjects of your first paragraph and you can put any plays, films or staged readings you've done into this portion of the bio. You can also use this section to promote your work in other areas of the industry. If you also write, direct, design or produce, your bio is the one and only place to make note of it. Never put these credits on your acting resume.

Paragraph 4 completes the picture of you, the person, with mentions of your interests, hobbies, professional affiliations, volunteer work, travel and home. Don't be shy here. Most actors have wide ranging interests and are adept at many things; that's why they can portray other people and activities convincingly. Sell yourself and what truly makes you unique.

You may be surprised to find that people will often connect with you because of what they've read in the last paragraph of your resume. Do not, however, include political and religious causes or mention a spouse and children. Let this be about you and no one else.

It can feel awkward to write without the use of "I" but a bio must be written in the third person. Vary the way in which you refer to yourself, always beginning with your full, professional name and then use just the first or last, rather than your full name in each paragraph:

Tracy Roberts most recently starred in…
Ms. Roberts graduated from the Yale School of Drama….
Tracy was honored to have been nominated for…
Roberts, a native of Tucson, is a member of …..

Print your bio on the same paper as your resume and trim it to the 8x10 size for a uniform presentation. Use the same logo designed for your resume at the top of your bio but include more photos if you have them.

When interviewing with an agent or manager, review your bio as though it were a study guide. It contains all the sound bites needed to answer most of the questions that will be asked of you with aplomb and assurance. If you're asked for a bio by a publicist for personal information for promotional purposes, handing over a professional bio practically guarantees they will find a way to feature you and your biographical hooks in press placements because you've done half the work for them. You have the total package defined and ready to go. That puts you ahead of the pack.

REELS AND DEMOS

Voice over demos and clip reels of film, television, or commercial work must be professionally edited and then duplicated on CD or DVD formats so you have them available to hand out at a go-see or meeting. For most auditions, you will submit reel and demo links via email. A demo should be one to two minutes long and a reel two to five minutes long. That's it. The only exception is when you have a great deal of professional work that crosses genres and you need to provide brief samples of all your recent jobs to an agent for an accurate idea of the extent of your bookings.

Start with the best sample clip (the listener/viewer may never go past it) and don't pad with transitional music, graphics or let your editor get artistic. Both voice and visual demos need to be crisply edited, featuring only your best work. Do not include voice or on-camera work that features other actors unless there is no way to edit them out or you are working with celebrity talent. Don't worry about on-camera clips relating the storyline; you're promoting your work, not the screenwriter's.

You should always have *j-cards,* the paper inserts that wrap around a DVD case or are inserted into a jewel case, with your logo and contact information as part of the packaging of each disk. You can print a brief paragraph outlining your recent, related credits directly on to the j-card so you don't have to include a separate cover letter with mailings. Office supply stores sell affordable kits for creating and printing j-cards on your home computer. These kits also contain labels for the cd/dvd, which should also contain your name, contact number, and a play list or you can purchase a labeler that prints directly on to CDRs, at computer stores.

Never say you have a reel or demo available if you don't; it takes time to assemble enough on camera work to create a reel and no one will penalize you for being at the start of your career even if you're older. If you do have a reel or demo, never go to an interview without a copy to leave with the director, agent or casting director. Always check each duplicate for glitches before distribution.

If you have interest in the voice over market but have yet to book an actual job, you can produce a spec demo of about six commercials in your own voice or character/ cartoon voices. Select copy that matches your castable voice types. Sometimes that can be a bit different from your on-stage/ on-camera types. If you're fluent in a foreign language with an accurate accent, consider doing one or two spots in that language. Voice over demos must have background music and sound effects professionally mixed and recorded for the purpose. They do not, however, require any special acting, voice or breath training beyond solid core techniques, with perhaps a few pointers regarding copy breakdown and microphone awareness, thrown in. If you are searching for a studio where you can record your demo and the owners insist that you pay for a pricey voice over course first, keep searching. They're ripping you off. One meeting with your regular coach to select copy (if you aren't confident choosing your own) and two or three coaching sessions to master the text is the most preparation any trained actor requires.

REVIEW SHEETS

If your work in films or on stage has been reviewed, or if your previous accomplishments were featured in publicity articles running in print or on-line publications, use these items to build a review sheet. These serve as a validation and amplification of your talent; hard copy that says you were worth hiring for the job or your work garners notice and publicity. If you've got these little gems, use them because they definitely catch the attention of agents, producers and casting directors.

Follow a few simple rules regarding the construction, design and usage of review sheets:

Every review segment must be attributed to both a critic/writer and the publication. You only need to include mentions that are relevant to your work, even if this is only a fragment.

Scan the publication's logo onto the review sheet for maximum impact with the review text beneath. Be certain that the project title is included or referenced in each mention.

Put the most important publication or reviewer first. If all your reviews are from lesser known publications but you have publicity pieces from major print, alternate between publicity and review with either the better known publication or best review taking precedence.

If you worked with name talent and they were also mentioned in the review, work their name into the quote by cobbling sentence fragments together: *"...Ms. Smith's stunning performance...directed by..."* or *"the film...a Sundance selection...."*.

Do a separate review sheet for each project in which you are personally reviewed if you have gathered enough usable material. This will serve to reinforce your excellence and marketability in that particular Castable Type. You can include a broader range of reviewers on these focused sheets. Include production stills if you have them.

If you have only a handful of good reviews accrued from many different projects then do one sheet that shows your consistent and continuing excellence across the board.

Use only the best reviews and the most recognizable publications or reviewers. Be sure to cite the name of each project within each review so that the reader knows to what the text refers.

Use alternate headshot or publicity photos to border or frame your review sheet: this is all about you so let your personality shine through.

Clip review sheets to your headshot and be sure to trim the sheet to the same size as your headshot, 8x10. Use the same paper as your resume for a sleek total package.

Use your review sheets when mailing headshots and re-sumes to agencies and casting offices for the first time. Don't resend these sheets unless you have added recent reviews. This is corroborating evidence of your talent and credits so use them accordingly. If you've scored those coveted positive notices don't let them languish in a scrapbook—put them to work!

WEB SITES AND SOCIAL MEDIA

Every actor should have an easy-to-navigate personal web site devoted solely to promoting themselves as a castable and successful acting professional.

You can use your personal website as a creative, interactive marketing tool, an on-line bio that audience, fans, press, peers, writers, producers, and directors can visit to find out more about you, the actor and your current and future projects. Use your bio for text and if you have a review sheet, include that, too but don't scan your resume onto the site. Resumes are focused strictly for the eyes of casting offices and agencies. Your web site will have a broader audience and should have more polish and panache.

Choose a domain name that includes your own professional name. If "yourname.com" is already taken, try "starringyourname.com". If you're non-union and haven't yet checked with SAG-AFTRA and/or AEA to see if your name is available, this would be a good time to do it.

Choose your best current photos as the main focus and add in a few, fun, candid or project related shots. Have a subscriber option so you can create a mailing list and keep friends and fans appraised of where they can see you perform. If you have enough work under your belt you could create a page for each major project or credit. But do keep the site easy to navigate and quick to load. Avoid long intros, video montages and overusing flash. Keep the site oriented toward your acting career. One professional photo of you with your kids or the dog is fine but the wedding photos and vacation snaps defeat the purpose of the site and take away from the professional image you've fostered. The same goes for blogs. If you want to blog, even about your work as an actor, it's safer to keep that separated from a promotional web site.

If you have short samples of voice over work you should definitely put them on your site. This is the one area where casting offices and agencies will accept a "submission by link,"so make sure the link is technically sound and the page containing your sample is clearly marked with the demo contents and your contact information.

Ask your alumni association, theater or film groups you are connected with to link to your site. Then spider your site for free on all the Internet search engines. Add your website address to your e-mail "signature." Network!

If you need the help of a web designer to build your website be sure to make arrangements for maintaining it as well. There are as many out-of-work web designers as there are out-of-work actors so you may find it more affordable than you anticipated or that a barter of services will suffice. Just don't allow your site to sit there with outdated information or broken links. If you don't feel that you can stay on top of a web site, don't launch one. But if you do, you'll probably find that it will become your favorite marketing tool and will introduce you to a world of artists you may never have otherwise met. Social media sites like Facebook can also be used as a promotional website as long as you create the page as an artist, not as a personal page. All the same guidelines apply, including selecting a personalized URL. While most people visit these sites regularly and there is no cost to creating a page, there are limitations to what you can do on a Facebook page and the rules and privacy policies are always changing. I recommend having both a personalized website as well as a dedicated Facebook page that can direct visitors to your website.

MAILINGS AND POSTCARDS

Once you've assembled a library of professional marketing materials you can begin a regular schedule of industry mailings.

There are many reasons for sending mailings:
- initial mailings at the start or re-start of your career
- making or continuing a contact
- distributing new or updated marketing material
- informing contacts of your current projects
- thanking contacts for attending a show or holding a meeting

Examples of what to include in a mailing:
Initial Mailing to Agents and Managers: headshot and resume, cover letter on letterhead and a demo or review page if you have them available.

Initial Mailing to Casting Directors: headshot and resume, review pages if you have them available, and a demo if the office accepts them.

Follow up Mailing to Agents and Casting Directors: postcards or show postcards with an invitation to current projects.

Thank you to Agent for attending performance: letter on logo stationery with review sheet if available. Cover letters are one of the simplest parts of a mailing. These should be brief and to the point. Follow the same guidelines used in writing postcards but use your logo letterhead and clip the note to your headshot.

POINTS TO REMEMBER:

- When making or continuing a contact reference the means of contact and reference your reason for mailing.
- When sending out project announcements be sure your "logo" appears on the announcement and spell out the specifics of your work in the project.
- No papers larger than the size of your headshot (8x10)

- Vary the picture used when possible.
- Always reference your current project.
- Think minimal, write simply, and be friendly.
- Triple check spelling, addresses, dates, etc.
- Keep accurate records of your mailings in a note-book specifically for that purpose.

Postcards are also a necessary part of your marketing package. They keep your name, face, and recent accomplishments in front of agents and casting director's. Once an agency or casting office has your current headshot and resume it is unnecessary and prohibitively expensive to continually resend it. Postcards are the method of choice for keeping your name, face and, most importantly, accomplishments, in front of the industry. Because they're smaller and sent out frequently to your contacts you should use several different shots or looks on the postcards to avoid constant repetition. Use the fun shots that wouldn't always be appropriate as 8x10 submissions but don't stray from the Castable Types you've been marketing.

There's never much room on postcards to write messages so always keep it accomplishment oriented: "I just booked a commercial for...." or "I was called back for...." and "... am currently in rehearsal for..." Don't be shy about what constitutes an accomplishment. Meeting with a respected agent, callbacks, a favorable notice, getting a reading with an important casting office are just a few examples of what will get noticed on the back of your postcard. What you write in your brief message should make the reader think, "why aren't I representing this actor?" or "if others in this business are seeing something in this actor, I want to meet him, too" or "this actor is starting to make headway, it's time for my office to go see her work." If your message doesn't convey a subtext of success, it's junk mail. Omit personal greetings, holiday wishes, and chatty missives. These may be postcards but they're still professional, business correspondence. Legibly sign your name at the bottom of your message for a friendly, personalized touch, especially if your mailing is going to a contact you've already met.

You can easily produce neat, large quantities of messages if you use sheets of 4"x 3" multi-purpose labels and your printer. When applied vertically to the back of the postcard they still leave room for an address label, stamp and postal marks.

Send out postcards every six to eight weeks, more frequently if you have something special to announce such as an appearance on a television show, a new commercial breaking or an opening. If you are appearing in a project that has its own postcards but your photo isn't on them, do a mailing of your postcards first, announcing the project and your work in it and then follow up later with a second mailing using the project's marketing materials. You first, the project second.

If your latest gig is a small indie project with little budgeted for marketing or they're using a generic postcard service to create mailers, consider making your own postcards for a limited mailing to your top industry contacts. Feature your name and photo as prominently as all the show information. When designed with a bit of creativity and printed on good quality paper, this can be a terrific, low cost, eye-catching solution for promoting your work in a labor of love. Don't send out the show postcard with your name circled in yellow highlighter and your own photo postcard stapled or paper clipped together in an envelope. If you received that in the mail you'd toss it in the trash, too. Remember, if the message on your postcard or letter isn't conveying a subtext of success, it's junk mail.

Getting a handle on the art of promoting your work in a way that gets noticed and brings results is the essence of marketing your talent. The effects will be immediate, placing you head and shoulders above actors. You'll feel much more confident in auditions and interview situations and will be treated with more respect by agents who appreciate clients who understand the importance of marketing materials and make their job just a little easier.

PART II:

Maximizing Your Acting Success

CHAPTER 8

DEFINING SUCCESS

The first step on the path to success and a core principle for taking charge of your career is defining your concept of success and what you aim to achieve as an actor. When you first started acting, your goals probably consisted of simply getting hired and not screwing up your lines. If you got paid, reimbursed for expenses or treated to drinks afterward, that was a bonus. You just wanted to act, to be considered a member of the creative community. You bounced from gig to gig with little thought of laying career foundations or care if you were moving forward, sideways or backward. As long as you were doing something, anything, it would eventually lead to that big break and keep your family and friends off your back.

Without well-defined goals as markers to guide and inform your art and choices along the path of an *enduring career*, you will eventually drift off course. Encountering realities, setbacks and the inevitable character building experiences can so deflate and derail you that staying on the road to success becomes untenable. You quickly find that the gig or agent or salary that once seemed to denote success isn't all that meaningful or exciting. Success is malleable. It changes with time and tide. The drama school you so desperately wanted to attend shows its limitations after a few semesters. The play gets mediocre reviews and sparse audiences. The agent who agreed to freelance for you takes headshots from anyone that walks through their door. Your television spot is edited down to one line and a reaction shot. The film that was going to get you noticed never gets distribution and no one ever sees it. You worked so hard to reach *these* goals yet in the end they don't make you feel the way you thought they would; you don't feel like a success. You probably made a lot of compromises in other areas of your life to attain this level of professional work and what do you have to show for it?

What you *should* have to show for it are stepping stones to continued and future success: a professional history of accomplishment, attaining creative goals, growth as an actor and achieving an ever increasing level of artistry and recognition, forming the lifeline of a career.

Setting goals creates direction and pace, giving you a manageable, marketable career that is directed in the course *you* choose. This allows you to attain cherished dreams, continuing on to the next one with the assurance and confidence that comes with achievement and mastery. Each goal realized is a building block to a life of success and not a means to an end.

YOUR DEFINITION

A single goal cannot define career success. It is one accomplishment in a life's work. Actors operate under the notion that one big break or one choice role will ensure a successful career. No job lasts forever and actors outgrow their parts. Tastes change and personal commitments transform the fabric of life. It can take years to establish your career and book work regularly. That one celebrated job can hang from your neck like an albatross if you don't have a next step on the horizon.

Begin to consider a bigger picture: a lifetime of goals and career of successes. This will be made up of a series of acting jobs and take many forms. Consider which genres fire your imagination, what makes you most excited about performing, who are the people you would like to work with, what kind of film and theatre do you *pay* to see, when does your creativity flow with the greatest ease? Honest answers to these questions can help you move away from what actors are expected to want and take you in the direction of what you truly desire.

LET YOUR GOALS MATURE WITH YOU

If you're working under a definition of success that is not yours and yours alone, your career will inevitably disappoint you; likewise if you never allow your goals to mature. Parents and coaches, for instance, can push you to be in the kind of entertainment they prefer and tend to consider markers of success. That influence may have felt supportive early on but stifling years later. Your initial dreams of being in commercial theatre may have soured upon realizing what is mostly produced is geared to the tastes of tourists. You don't care to see those shows let alone be in them. You may have grown to the point where you would rather be in films you write and direct, focusing all your energy into personal expression and a unique point of view, or you may have discovered that commercials and print work are what you most enjoy doing: they bring recognition and good income and leave you plenty of energy and resources to pursue other interests or avant garde productions.

This is inevitable, normal career growth but is not always embraced by actors. The fear that the only measure of success is commercial recognition in highly visible mainstream projects keeps actors from growing, exploring, and maturing. No one thinks twice when an attorney tires of practicing law and moves to another discipline such as teaching law or politics, orwhen a teacher decides the classroom no longer holds sway and leaves to write the great American novel. You, too, can explore all the options that are open to you without failing as an actor. In many ways, actors have it better than people in other professions as the competition for roles in highly visible shows decreases as one gets older and the ability to compete for roles in big budget productions grows with age. Think of this as an insurance policy for your acting career and you may feel safe enough to explore your creativity earlier and with more gusto and abandon.

GET REAL, GET FOCUSED

What are your creative and career goals as an actor for the season ahead, the year to come and five years into the future? What would make you feel as though you had grown your talent and ability to express and use it? How will you expand your share of the acting market through the uniqueness that is your Castable Types? Write these down. Give your aspirations shape and form. This is a simple exercise and yet profound and far reaching as it can take you anywhere you want to go. This will be the basis of your career plan, so start now and be true to yourself. Keep in mind that your plan for a successful acting career is based on *your* needs, hopes and dreams. Cast aside childish, star struck notions about the industry and fame as a substitute for achievement and success. It is not. This isn't your parent's career or a reality show where your moods and whims are crafted into entertainment. Foolish ideas about your career, just like dated methods of acting training, will not help you.

PROCESS BEFORE OUTCOME

Ask an actor what his or her career goals are for the year ahead and you'll usually hear, "I want to get out there," "I want to book something" or "I just want to get paid to act." Hardly the markers of achievement and growth one should be striving to attain.

This thinking is self-defeating because it focuses on outcomes rather than on living a professional, artistic life. Of course, you should set and strive to achieve goals and enjoy the outcome when fully realized. But those outcomes are the results of the process of living, being and working as an actor every day. No one outcome is going to make a process feel worthwhile. If you hate what you do on a daily basis to reach the outcome, no amount of success will make up for that. If your life is a constant cycle of stress, frustration and unhappiness booking a high profile role on occasion will not make up for the time spent living through a miserable process. You may believe that the end will more than make up for the means and the misery will be forgotten in the glow of your work being seen for a time. Once that job is over, you'll be back in the struggle and grind, chasing after the next temporary gain.

RETHINK

Stop thinking about your acting career in foolish ways. You've been thinking about it, stressing over it, wrestling with it and possessed by it for years. How far has that gotten you? It's time to rethink your career; consider it from an entirely different point of view, a point of view that will make decisions easier to reach, choices less stressful and remove the anxiety and loathing from the endless cycle of auditions and interviews.

Approach your career as if you were the CEO of your own small company. In reality, you are. You are an independent contractor, a small business owner who pitches a product – your talent and creativity – to other companies and, when successful, lands the contract and does the job. You may be a member of a union, you may not; you may have arrived via professional referral - through an agent or manager - or you may have found the job on your own. But any way you slice it, you are a business owner. You have to finance and tend to the business of your acting career. The sooner you start rethinking your career from that perspective, the sooner you'll achieve success.

OWNER AND CEO

As the Owner and CEO of the company (your acting career), you should be aware that some behaviors and strategies simply don't fly in the business world. It's not that business whizzes don't think outside of the box, on the contrary; creativity in your field is prized and rewarded. But when it comes to mapping out a business plan for career success there are some tacks that are proven winners and some that always lead to disaster. Disaster is expensive. Disaster costs capital: creative, emotional, financial and physical capital. Most small businesses have finite amounts of these resources so their careful and considered allocation is key. Avoiding these disastrous choices allows you more leeway when taking considered risks and keeps you from looking like a total fool. It can also extend the life of your company as most small businesses fail in the first few years.

So what should you *not* be doing?

Don't:

- Take career advice from people outside the field such as your psychic, hairdresser, spirit guide or life coach.

- Take career advice from unsuccessful people in the field including your roommate, significant other, spouse, best friend, psychic, hairdresser, spirit guide or life coach.

- Allow your family to limit your Castable Types based on *their* definition of you.

- Learn acting technique through classes taught by casting directors or agents.

- Allow photographers to design the "product" packaging when they don't even know what the product is.

- Set unrealistic deadlines for attaining unrealistic goals.

- Put all your *financial* capital into one venture, such as headshots, and then have nothing left with which to operate.

- Put all your *emotional* capital into one venture, such as getting an agent or a particular role, and when it doesn't work out have nothing left with which to operate.

- Believe that famous teachers or classes will bring you success if you just spend enough time and money taking them.

- Allow people to tell you that your product is no good and will never be successful.

In other words, stop running around desperately seeking advice from anyone who feels like giving it or gets off on telling you what to do and expects you to pay them for the privilege; these people can't wait for your needy butt to show up so they can feel superior to somebody, anybody, and make a few bucks while doing it. Stop letting your family (who never really thought you would still be pursuing acting at this point and don't understand why the industry views you as something other than what they know you to be) make you feel bad about your choices; they're going to have to get used to the fact that their *baby* may portray someone who has sex, does drugs, gets naked, looks bad and doesn't always get paid much to do it. Stop sharing with your competition. No matter what the roommate, friend or lover says to you about chasing different markets or being different types, no one ever wants to be the least successful of the pair and will take every opportunity to engage in subtle forms of sabotage. Stop buying into the empty promises of those lousy studio schools that try to pass off buying access to an agent or casting director as a shortcut to success. It isn't. You won't learn a thing or book a job by presenting yourself as an untrained actor who needs a class to learn to read five lines from some crappy sitcom script that never got picked up by the network. Stop letting photographers tell you what your headshots should look like: being a headshot photographer is not synonymous with being a career coach. If that photographer has never seen you act and has lost all perspective on talent from hanging out with bony, brain-dead models, his or her opinion is useless anyway. Stop working dead-end survival jobs that fill you with frustration, cut off your career connections and make you feel like a loser just so you can save up for overpriced headshots. Once you get them, you're totally unprepared to use them, because you haven't had the time or energy to work on your acting or audition skills. You can't afford a class or coach because you spent all your money on headshots. Stop paying top dollar to study with a famous teacher or a teacher of someone famous because you think that success will rub off on you or that doors will open because of the connection. As they say in the diet drug ads "*results not typical – your results may vary.*" Stop telling yourself that if you don't get your union card, an agent or starring role on Broadway, network television or a studio film by the end of the year, you're a failure. This is your career and not a crash diet; you need to plan for the long haul, for long-term success. Besides, union cards and agents have never conferred professional viability or guarantees of success. The world is littered with the acting equivalent of one-hit wonders. One big, splashy job doesn't make a career but, in fact, can kill it. So can making these mistakes repeatedly. Any CEO who would run a business in this way, without a plan for the future, exposing his product to detriment and wasting vast amounts of money would be fired. Yet these are mistakes everyone makes at one time or another. Being an actor doesn't absolve you from having to support yourself or your career. You are allowed to have an aptitude for business without destroying your creativity. In fact, when your brain is firing on all cylinders, your creativity and your career will start to gel.

CHAPTER 9

THE ACTOR AS CEO:
DESIGNING YOUR CAREER PLAN

SURVIVAL JOB SYNDROME

The world is filled with many talented and intelligent actors. Performers who are the acting equivalent of baseball's five-tool player: they act, write, sing, direct and originate projects from the ground up, extraordinarily artistic, multi-faceted actors: creative, educated and aching to perform, yet most remain completely unknown to audiences and industry alike. No one sees the work of these inspired people. Their talent and artistic soul is trapped in the life of a waiter and can't get out. Their existence, in which acting and artistry are never integrated into their daily lives or given ample opportunity to shine on stage or screen, causes a disconnect from creativity and professional connections, derailing success, fostering desperation and denying long sought dreams.

They are the actors caught in *Survival Job Syndrome.*

THE BEST OF INTENTIONS

Leslie worked for a catering company; a job she took thinking it would enable her acting career with its flexible schedule and low level demands. Most of her co-workers were actors, too and someone always seemed to be on the verge of booking a job in the next big thing or have important connections she hoped to share. Celebrities and industry types frequented many of the events and parties she worked which, at first, made her feel connected, however tenuously, to the entertainment world. At a few occasions she had brief conversations with industry stars who always complimented her good looks and great figure, telling her to hang in there. With hard work and a little luck, someone would give her a shot. Being a waiter-caterer wasn't the greatest job in the world but it felt like the tried and true path of the striving actor. Besides, she didn't know of any other way to approach her career.

Graduating with a BFA in drama four years earlier, Leslie struggled to stay afloat. Every penny she earned went right back out to pay for the basics of life and little more. A series of flaky roommates often left her stuck with the entire rent bill, blowing the few dollars she had saved. She could get a second job but the late nights her catering gig required kept her sleeping well past noon, leaving just enough time to make the last round at casting calls. Free time to audition for everything out there was a priority to Leslie. Being seen by everyone for everything, she reasoned, would better her chances of booking a gig: moving to a "real" job was out of the question. Working at anything 9 to 5 would be the same as giving up on acting and that wasn't going to happen. Money was always so tight though, she could barely afford to re-produce her headshots to leave at calls. She saved up to buy spots in agent nights at a studio school and take high-priced seminars with casting directors but nothing ever came of the expensive purchases. Not a single talent agency or casting director called her in for an interview or requested she leave them a few headshots and resumes. At work, Leslie would wonder how other actors she worked with survived, puzzled by those who were signed with agencies, but had practically no training and the frankly not so attractive people who always seemed to book commercial work.

Falling into the hole

It doesn't have to be a job waiting tables, tending bar or temping that traps you. Any job that devalues your creativity, underutilizes your talent and isolates you from your true aspirations can cause your acting career to slip away, sometimes for good. An actor's soul trapped in the life of a waiter or temp leads to self-defeating cycles of spending all one's financial and emotional capital on the *big move* that's supposed to make all the difference but rarely ever does. Whether it's the class taught by the casting director of the moment, new model-like headshots, or showcases mounted for agents to attend, the results are the same. And after that big buy amounts to nothing, it's back to the restaurant or temp agency for months of scraping by on the survival job and deeper depression.

BROKE-ASS REALITY

Depressed, Leslie would fall into total self-loathing when she thought about her dismal state: she never seemed to have enough money to support herself and her career, hated her dead end job but didn't want to commit to a full time schedule and give up on auditioning or acting. She couldn't stand being around other actors at work who complained continually about the industry and their agents, gossiped about one another and were competitive to the point of malice. Why were they so miserable when they at least had a few bites of the apple? Why were they so guarded with their connections when she was obviously a different type and could never be a competitive threat? The celebs to whom she served drinks and canapés and used to admire treated her like the hired help she was; no one ever made good on a promise of comps to screenings or previews and rarely ever tipped. Her costly "unused" fine arts degree and college success taunted her; she had been so successful in school, starring in productions of Shakespeare, important avant-garde plays and being selected for master classes with legendary guest teachers, but now she couldn't land background work in a commercial. Her only credits consisted of unpaid work in films shot without permits and the promise of deferred pay if they ever made it to a festival or got a distribution deal. She would be paying off her student loans for courses in mask work and historical styles for twenty years at this rate. The across the board rejection from agents and casting directors was the ultimate insult. Leslie, who started out with so much energy and enthusiasm, now felt like a failure as a performer and a person. She stopped telling people she was an actor. In her mind, she wasn't even a struggling actor because she hadn't performed in anything in almost two years. She was just a struggling waiter, who couldn't afford to see a movie or play, dreaded looking through *Backstage* and avoided talking about acting because it made her so depressed. When her family and friends would ask her when they would finally get to see her in something, she wanted to scream. Her boyfriend would often tell her he wished she'd do something else—something she could be successful doing, something that didn't hurt her so much so she wouldn't be so depressed and uptight all the time.

HITTING THE WALL

When actors have enough of their broke-ass reality and the pressure of feeling like a failure while having to defend career choices finally comes to a head, most give themselves the big ultimatum, the now or never move that's usually the final nail in the coffin of an acting career. It's the last audition, last mailing, last unpaid project they will do, unless they get some measure of success out of it. But one move, one project, no matter how it turns out, can't make up for years of missteps and desperation. Nor is it enough to keep building on long term. The inevitable decision to move on, whether made in one moment or allowed to simply happen, is usually just an angry denial of creativity though the need to express it often festers for years to come. This makes walking away from acting as painful for an actor as staying in the business.

When Leslie first contacted me for coaching, the desperation in her voice was palpable. The pressure she was putting herself under manifested itself as tension, freezing her entire body and coming out as nervous energy that ruined her cold reading and monologue work. She was uncomfortable performing in an audition setting and just being in her own skin. Anticipating rejection and second guessing everything she had learned, Leslie presented herself and her talent poorly. The attractive, well-educated actor, brimming with enthusiasm, was nowhere to be found. If this was the person showing up at casting calls it wasn't surprising that agents and casting directors were passing her over without a second thought. She was running herself ragged with absolutely no career plan; going to every and any call, putting herself in front of casting directors with no intention of booking her type or level of experience and no idea of how the industry viewed her or how she should market her talent to the industry. Leslie was adrift in a cycle of failure and it didn't have to be that way.

There were several components of Leslie's acting and audition technique, marketing and career planning that we worked together to improve but the first and most pressing matter to be tackled was getting her out of the morass of self-defeat and negativity she was mired in - her career had to stop sucking! I wanted her to banish the notion that the words starving and artist are inextricably linked. Leslie believed that, to be an actor, one is destined to be broke and un-empowered until the magical day you get your lucky break and an agent or casting director plucks you from obscurity, raw and unpolished, and reality changes. This was sabotaging Leslie's career as it has so many others. I had to cure Leslie of a big, bad case of *Survival Job Syndrome* so she could manage the day to day aspects of being a professional actor and move on to creating and implementing a plan of action for her acting career.

REALITY CHECK THE PRICE OF PASSION

We all have bills to pay and expenses to meet. Acting can be a lucrative profession even at levels shy of the fame and fortune accompanying major gigs. But it takes time to achieve consistent bookings with reliable income. During that period of establishment and reputation building many actors pull the rug out from under themselves. They take survival jobs believing they won't demand much of their time and talents, saving that energy for their acting and leaving flexibility to attend auditions. But when your day to day life is an emotional, intellectual and creative void, what are you doing to your artistic flow? Jobs that demand little of your talent and skills usually offer less in terms of pay and benefits so your basic needs may be getting met, but what's left over to invest in your acting career? Is the one aspect of your life you most want to nurture getting the shortest shrift? Can you really dash off to casting calls any time, or do supervisors and co-workers start to complain about your commitment to what you consider a temporary situation? Do you have money for gas or the subway to get to a call on time and be ready to shine? Are you really saving your energy for auditions, or is it being crushed under the weight of feelings that you're wasting your life in a lousy job at the bottom of the food chain? Networking? Forget about it. You're so far removed from the profession that reading the trades gives you anxiety attacks and you reek of desperation. You tell yourself to buckle down, work extra shifts, take a second job and save up so you can take a few months off and then really focus on auditioning, maybe get the new headshots with a celebrity photographer you know will change everything. Then you'll do a massive mailing to every address in *Call Sheet* and find a showcase and hope for the best. But when the time comes to make that break you can't do it. You still have bills to pay and those expensive headshots ate up all the extra money you stashed away. You take extended breaks from auditioning and attending class waiting until you get your life and career together until it's all perfect and foolproof; casting directors wouldn't know you from Adam, let alone show up to see you in a showcase or low budget film. You're not just stuck in the same place you were months or a year ago; you're doing even *less* acting work now than you were before. Just like Leslie, you're trapped in *Survival Job Syndrome*.

FROM PASSION TO PROFESSION

When you totally compartmentalize your acting career from the rest of your life it's like a stray shoe lost in the back of your closet. You're not progressing as an actor and you aren't even using your native intelligence or practical skills in a non-acting job that engages you or offers some level of fulfillment. You're drifting further away from your industry connections and friends and family start to wonder if you have secretly given up on your acting aspirations. At times you do, too. It's time to dig that shoe out from under the pile of dirty clothes and reunite it with its mate. Wear those magic slippers every day and get back to making acting the center of your life. If you've fallen victim to this syndrome the time to break free is now.

STOP DREAMING, START DOING

Your acting career is a business you own and operate; how will it ever grow and succeed if it's only attended to in your spare time with whatever funds are left over after paying the bills?

Being an actor shouldn't mean living a clichéd existence of noble poverty and suffering for your art at a job you hate. Acting doesn't have to be a life of financial struggle and professional marginalization for the rare reward of speaking someone else's words.

Approach your career from the perspective of a business owner, integrating it into your entire life. You will achieve more tangible results, get out of survival mode and enjoy acting once again. Designing a career plan of action leading to the realization of your personal definition of acting success and the attainment of your desired goals is the proven way to make your wishes become the reality of a fulfilling and expansive career.

The acting industry has so many variables that most actors believe it is impossible to make and follow through on a plan of action in a realistic way. That thinking is uninformed and un-empowering. Yes, acting is a tough business and many decisions are out of your hands. But an equal number are in your hands and it's up to you to take charge of what you can. You can either run your career or run after your career. It's your choice. You are the owner and CEO of your acting career. You have creative, financial and emotional capital to invest in your career. You have a unique product, your Castable Types and a core marketing strategy is required to get the right segment of the industry to become aware of and interested in your product. Next, you build your brand. You need to plan, make informed decisions and execute your strategy for success to make your capital investment pay off long term. The power to see your plan of action through always lies in your hands.

PLANNING POINT #1 - VALUING YOUR TALENT AND CREATIVITY

Leslie wasn't dealing with her financial life because it set off feelings of failure and panic. When she needed to spend money to further her acting career, it would turn into the financial emergency of the moment, something new for her to stress over.

Like most actors, Leslie never considered her career a business or that her talent and drive could create income that would complement her acting. She never took the time to think about the dollars or planning required to keep her career/business operating. She felt marginalized and treated her career with a similar sense of disdain. She no longer felt worthy as an artist and in turn, didn't want to waste any more money on acting. Yet, here she was in my studio for one last try.

Under-Utilizing Your Talent

Many actors willingly assume the role of starving artist, starving their talent as well. If the only way you can make ends meet is with a restaurant, sales or office job that's fine, but don't let that non-creative job take over your life, imagination and energy. Don't let it become a steel-jawed trap around your ankle that defines you as something other than an actor.

I wanted Leslie to reconnect on a regular basis with the creativity she so carefully nurtured in school and reignite her love of acting. She thrived as an actor in college because she was focused on performing and the majority of her time and energy was devoted to that. Now her focus was waiting tables. When I asked her about the college courses she most excelled in and really loved, mask work came up repeatedly, something she thought was strictly academic and esoteric with no practical application in her career. We discussed several ways she could bring the art of masks back into her world, deciding a blog on the subject was the best way to begin. Leslie wrote and posted three short articles on mask performance and history, using a Creative Commons license to post drawings from old texts and included photos of masks she had used in performance. Far from being busy work, the blog opened up a well spring of lost creativity in her acting and challenged her intellectually. Getting back in touch with the physical demands and grace of mask work released the physical tension that was flattening her cold readings and monologues at auditions.

Another client of mine, who was a close friend of a puppet and performance art master performing in a critically acclaimed Off-Broadway show at the time set, Leslie up with comp tickets and an introduction to the show's creator. He gave her an interview and photos to post on the blog which drove a lot of traffic to the site. Among those who visited the blog were several teachers who invited Leslie to speak to their art classes and two film makers, one used Leslie's own drawings of masks in a series of animated web shorts and the other cast Leslie in two of his independent films: her first two screen credits and her first paid acting job.

Leslie had begun the process of reclaiming her identity as a performer, her drive and her love of acting. She had begun to network with people in the industry who were commercially successful and well-connected and valued her talents and artistic point of view. This opened the doors to acting work and parallel work opportunities: ways in which she could earn money while making full use of her artistry.

Feed Your Starving Artist's Soul

Leslie's story is a great example of why you must never let your off-hours consist solely of a weekly cold reading class with a bunch of other depressed actors, or drinks with co-workers spent bitching about your boss. You may be a starving artist but don't starve your artistry—do something! Avoid getting distracted by the little dramas and triumphs of your survival job. When you have breaks between acting jobs take a college level drama lit or cinema studies course and renew your creativity. Get involved with the board of a theatre company, film center, arts related charity or create your blog. Keep the avenue of expression for your personal sense of artistry alive and open. Far from being busy work, this is how you attract the people that could one day invest in your next project, bring media contacts to your plays and screenings, or nominate you for awards and grants. This is one way to get to know the people who really sustain the creative community and for them to know you—not as a struggling actor who waited their table last week, but as a true multi-faceted artist; the type of actor who isn't merely chasing fame, but has something to contribute to the cultural landscape and is worth following. Involvements like these, allowing you to use your other talents, perhaps designing or writing, can lead to creative jobs which complement and integrate with your acting, paying as much as the office gig but with far more fulfillment. At the very least, this interface will balance out that soul-numbing survival job and give perspective to the hours spent not acting. Successful business owners know that involvement in trade and network-ing organizations, as well as social clubs and activities, are the best ways to make connections, get new ideas and stay on top of trends. This principle is as true for the actor as it is for the boutique owner.

Too many actors hide their career choice and creative point of view for fear of being judged a failure. You must be an unsuccessful actor if you have to work at other jobs to meet your bills or worse, you must not be a very good ac-tor, right? Wrong! Any working actor can tell you that's not the truth. It takes time to create new projects, you can wait six to eight weeks for the check from that voice over to hit your mail box and some union contracts pay less than a shift manager's job at a fast food restaurant. Still, the rent has to be dealt with during that gestation period. There's only so much *paid* acting work out there and many people may be an apt choice to fill a single role but only one person can be hired. You may be very good, but not the one who ultimately books the job. The project you're working on may be worthy but doesn't make it. This is the way the professional arena operates, and not just in the realm of acting. Every small business person strives for consistency in income but achieving that level takes time, experience and establishing a track record of prior success. Small business owners have months where they don't meet their sales quotas, attorneys lose cases and web designers have dry spells with no new clients. It's not just actors who struggle and have to find ways to supplement their cash flow. Nevertheless, actors will take their tough patches so personally that they stop being actors and go into hiding, re-emerging only when they have figured out how to have the perfect career. When was the last time you met a lawyer who, after losing a few judgments, no longer considered herself an attorney, vowing to resume practice only when she knows every case can be won? Absolutely ridiculous ways of thinking, but actors fall into this trap all the time.

Planning Point #2 - Finance Your Career

We now moved on to the next survival issue: financing her acting career. The fact that Leslie didn't have a big income could no longer be used as an excuse for shutting down her career. If acting was going to be her business she could no longer ignore the financial realities of supporting her career or she would never achieve progress. We began by making a list of all the business-related expenses Leslie needed to cover over the course of a calendar year:

- photo shoot and stylist, hair and makeup mainte-nance
- reproducing headshots

- professional wardrobe
- creating and copying resumes
- coaching, workshops and showcases
- envelopes and postage
- transportation
- scripts and trade publications
- show/movie tickets

We added up the cost of all these work-related expenses and divided the total by 12. This gave us the working figure she would need to have available to spend on her acting career each month. Instead of feeling overwhelmed by the cost of getting headshots and having to come up with the $700 needed all at once, Leslie would be reserving a portion of that outlay each month so she would have the money available when she needed it. This put an end to losing sleep trying to figure out how to finance her career out of her next two paychecks and still cover rent.

In Leslie's case, she needed to set aside approximately $565.00 a month to cover her planned acting expenses over a twelve month period. This figure would enable her to have weekly coaching sessions, participate in two industry showcases during pilot seasons, get headshots and have them reproduced with the money to mail them out and get to auditions. By Leslie's calculations, she was already spending, on average, close to $275.00 a month on acting-related expenses like transportation, resumes, postage and grooming. Less than half of what she needed to properly finance her career at this stage.

Her initial reaction to covering the monthly shortfall was panic. The additional $290.00 she needed each month was a lot of money to Leslie and she didn't want to take on a second job or work seven days a week to make up the difference. Looking at the gap in her acting budget in another light, she could see it was only $72.00 a week or about $10.00 a day more that she had to find or earn somehow. We could certainly find ways to trim a few extraneous expenses in other areas and make up the rest with a little ingenuity.

Leslie had converted a one bedroom apartment into two bedrooms. She rented out the original bedroom to roommates and slept in the smaller room, with a lot of her belongings spilling out into the communal living room. We flipped that arrangement because she could charge more for the "two room" half of the apartment. She wasn't even home most nights and weekends because of her work schedule so this was a minor inconvenience, allowing her to charge $175.00 more per month in rent. Her next roommate was required to sign a lease agreement and leave a security deposit so she wouldn't get stuck in another desperate situation. As basic as all this seems, these were details Leslie overlooked because she was always in a state of panic and never in charge of her life or career.

We found the remaining $115.00 needed each month by cutting back on the number of auditions Leslie went to each week. She was wasting her time and money going to calls for projects she had no chance of booking (she needed to target her auditions more carefully to suit her Castable Types) and taking full advantage of the meals she was entitled to when working as a waiter-cater. She usually skipped those freebie feasts and would buy food on her way home after work, which added up. Leslie now made a point of taking full advantage of one of the few perks her job had to offer.

Each month, Leslie put aside any unused money from her acting budget so the cash for big expenditures would be there when she needed it. She could fund her career without taking the dreaded 9 to 5 job or working seven days a week. With her short term money issues under control, we could turn our attention to creating a career plan of action for Leslie so she could achieve her career goals and start experiencing real success.

Planning Point #3 - Intelligent Goal Setting

Like all actors, Leslie had goals she wanted to achieve in her career. Securing representation so she could audition for professional jobs was one of them. Creating her plan of action to get a commercial agent gave us the perfect opportunity to learn the skill of intelligent goal setting.

First, we clarified the type of representation she needed for the markets in which she wanted to work. That means, if an actor's sole focus is theatre, pursuing commercial agents would be a waste of time. If an actor is new to the industry, a top agency may not be interested until a few solid credits are on the resume. In Leslie's case, she chose to focus on commercials, print and voice over since it's a busy market, with plenty of non-union work. She needed to target the agencies that handle those areas. I advised Leslie that freelancing with several agencies would be the best way to go so she had the most opportunities to get audition slots.

A mass mailing to every agency in town was not an effective use of Leslie's financial and emotional capital. She wanted to throw everything she had to use against the wall in one big gesture to see what would stick. I knew that such a move would leave her depressed and diminished when she had few or any responses and she would want to give up. A focused, well thought out and researched approach would bring her better results while allowing Leslie to stay viable in the industry longer. Her capital resources would not be wasted.

ACTION PLANNING EXAMPLE: FINDING REPRESENTATION

Whether you want to find an agent or prepare for a headshot shoot, begin bysetting a series of goals within manageable time frames that include the steps and tasks required to reach your objectives. Using three month, six to nine month and one year periods is optimal. Think of what you need to accomplish to make each time frame a building block toward your definition of success. Let's continue with the goal of finding representation. You want to work with an agent as soon as possible who will get you auditions for television, commercials and voiceover work. What are the specific steps you need to take to accomplish that and how long will it take you to complete each step? Plot it out.

Step One: Research Agents in this field with whom you could work

Who works with union or non-union talent, who takes a chance on new actors, who works mostly with established actors?

Look for information online or in the trades about these agents and the actors they represent to gain insight into the agent's taste and sensibility. An insider tip I will share with you is to check out the websites of actors represented by a particular agent or manager to get an idea of the level of talent he or she represents, if there are other actors who look like you or have similar training and experience. You'll be surprised how much you can glean from this little investment of time.

Step Two: Make a targeted mailing list of the agents that will work with you

You may be targeting individuals at an agency that you have met or targeting the agency itself. Keep notes on this so if an agent moves to a new company or the agency merges with another office, you know who you are following. These changes happen often.

Step Three: Assemble your marketing materials

Your Castable Types headshot, resume, and other appropriate marketing materials should be ready to go into an envelope and mailed.

Always double check reels, make sure all contact information is correct and that your mailing is neat and professionally put together.

Step Four: Make a mailing calendar as part of your marketing plan

One mailing is not enough. The industry needs to know you are available to work consistently and to read about your professional accomplishments. It's up to you to do it.

Schedule the dates your regular mailings should go out in your calendar.

Also note the midpoint between each mailing date. Use that midpoint as a reminder that you need to get a fresh Castable Type relevant accomplishment to your credit to use on your next postcard mailing.

Stay on schedule. Keep those postcard mailings going for your selected time period.

Step Five: Make Contact

Look for well-produced industry showcases with panelists who are on your targeted mailing list or agents and casting directors who are actively seeking talent. Don't waste capital on showcases with thirty actors reading assigned cold copy.

Step Six: Review and revise

You may not get personal responses from the majority of agents you mail to but that doesn't mean they aren't looking at your photos or making note of your accomplishments. Don't cut anyone from your list that is still a good match for your talent and goals for at least 12 months.

Make notes on anyone who does call you in for an interview or watches your work in a showcase. You may want to tailor future mailings to these contacts in response to your meeting. For instance, if you meet with an agent based on your mailing and a concern is raised over your on-camera experience, a follow up mailing may point out that you are in a professional level on-camera class, have booked a small role in a film or contain a brief demo reel of your work in spec commercials.

Stay Positive and patient. Your targeted mailing is a marketing campaign for your talent. It takes time to build your brand.

You now have a six steps action plan for achieving the goal of securing commercial representation. Within these six clearly defined steps you have added benefits that will improve other aspects of your career. Step One is targeting a market that you want to pursue, that focuses your talent and attention. Step Two familiarizes you with a segment of the business, commercial agents and raises your industry savvy while building a contact list. Step Three requires that you always have the appropriate Castable Type marketing materials ready to use and have budgeted for their creation. Step Four require that you stay committed to your career and goals and always be pursuing new accomplishments. Step Five puts you in front of the people who can get you auditions and book you for jobs, make new contacts, network and get over audition and performance anxiety. Step Six allows you to see your progress as an acting professional, identify weaknesses and strengths in your marketing materials and plan. That's a lot of benefit from one segment of your action plan. By listing the specific steps and recognizing the benefits of completing each one, then actually following your plan, your efforts reverberate across every aspect of your acting career.

I've used a targeted agent mailing as an example of intelligent goal setting within a plan of action. You should repeat this process with every goal that you have for your career for the year ahead. Keep your objectives clear by writing out each goal and its steps separately then look at them all side by side. Look for the points where benefits overlap to keep yourself motivated and help create a logical order for tackling your list. Be aware that some goals take longer to achieve, while others can be completed in short order once the steps are laid out in front of you. Assign dates to start or repeat steps rather than due dates. Once you get in the habit of starting and feeling the progress you are making, *done* dates will come naturally and allow for flexibility doors, open and opportunities appear. When obstacles do seem to be in your way, don't fixate on them. Look to your earlier steps to see where you can find an alternate path to work around the perceived barrier. Review your missteps and progress regularly to keep your plan of action sharp and fresh and become aware of how intelligent goal setting within a career plan of action protects and increases your artistic flow.

167

THE JOYS OF OWNERSHIP

Let your fear of selling out your dreams, being unsuccessful, feeling like an outsider, unwanted or of just plain failing, slip away. When you release those outdated, negative, self-defeating beliefs about being an actor you hold deep inside, you allow something wonderful to emerge. You allow a new confidence about your ability, talent, and identity as an actor to rise to the surface: a healthier, realistic and positive mindset that gives you the strength to break free from Survival Job Syndrome and move forward as a successful, working actor. What you do to pay the bills is what you do to pay the bills, not who you are or the limit to what you may achieve. Seek parity between the number of hours you spend at the office and the hours you spend developing your acting career. Eventually, the latter will become as lucrative as the former and you can rely on regular income from acting. In the interim, be an integrated actor—an actor whose artistic life force is always present in their work and who finds inspiration in everyday events and interactions.

When you live your life as an actor and an artist, at all times, your creativity becomes a positive, purposeful force that is readily accessed and applied at all times. Stifling that force, that easy *flow* allowing emotional connection to your work, shuts you down as a performer. That flow will set you apart from the rest of the actors on the scene, so protect and nurture your creative connection through integrative career planning, acknowledging your talents and presenting yourself as an actor to everyone you know. Step out of the morass of Survival Job Syndrome, leave the crappy classes and crappier gigs behind and stop banging your head against the wall. Make wise use of your creative and financial capital, seize ownership of your talent and your take charge of your acting career.

CHAPTER 10

STRATEGIES OF SUCCESSFUL ACTORS

If, after reading this book, you are excited to bring your unique talent and energy to your acting through your Castable Types and are ready to take charge of your career, there are several strategies you can use to help make your dream a reality. These success principles can keep you from making foolish mistakes, falling into self-defeating habits, overcome adversity and generate forward momentum.

COMMITMENT TO THE JOURNEY

As you now know, a life in acting is a journey that must be embraced and managed as it will never be perfect, never be *done*. Striving for career perfection is a form of creative suicide. Nothing in life is ever perfect, no matter how much planning or money you throw at the endeavor. Just ask any newlywed who spent eighteen months putting together a dream wedding. You're never going to be at the point where you book every job, play only award worthy roles, residual checks rolling in and great reviews piling up. That just isn't going to happen. It doesn't happen for anyone. You may go through periods where your agent is putting you up for the right gigs and casting directors love you, but you aren't booking. You may be a brilliant actor but agencies aren't repping you because they already have several of your type on their rosters at the moment.

You alone are responsible for your career success. Even with the best professional support system, a well-considered career plan, solid technique and a wealth of talent, it's still up to you to attain your goals. You have to make the personal commitment to honor your talent and make it available for the world to see. You have to make the journey. The rigors of mastering your craft and developing your personal artistry soon become the daily grind of mailings and interviews and auditions. When bookings don't follow or the projects you do land flop, it can become overwhelming. But that is the reality of professional life, not just in the entertainment business but in all professions. Attorneys, physicians, merchants, brokers, and athletes all experience professional loss and setbacks from time to time. Rarely do they let those setbacks derail their careers or destroy their confidence to the point of quitting. Rather, they learn from their mistakes and make adjustments, accept loss and continue to pursue their dreams. As a professional actor, the CEO of your own company, you must do the same. Take responsibility for running your acting career as a business, diligently practice the personal and contextual work that is the basis of the Castable Type Approach and Complete Thought Technique, make brave and thoughtful choices in performance, study great actors, read great plays, network, market and attend as many films and shows as possible. Then get up and do it all over again the next day. This is commitment. This is the only way to achieve real and lasting success. The only people who ever truly commit to their goals are those who believe they deserve success. There will always be someone who wants the job a little bit more: be that person. You won't book every gig but your work will be noticed, your approach respected. In time, you will be known as a talented pro, an actor's actor, a bankable hire.

With dedication and commitment, not judgments and fear, you will get past temporary blockages because that's all they are, temporary. Your acting career is a road to be traveled with many twists and turns. The key, as successful actors know, is to stay on track. Consistently successful actors don't get thrown off by obstacles and fall into the void that is negative thinking and desperate behavior. They don't let their acting careers slip away.

PATIENCE AND PERSPECTIVE

Just as you are not going to become a great actor over-night, or by taking a six week class or even a two year con-servatory program, you are never going to have all aspects of your career exactly where you want them at any one time. Often the reason is that success in one part of your career points out the deficiencies in other areas. As you begin to book better roles and are able to secure representation, you'll be submitted for more competitive, higher profile jobs and you're going to take a few steps back in terms of where you place next to a new level of competition. You'll have to further hone your audition skills and accept smaller roles to master success on a new rung of the ladder. This is an inevitable part of the career journey and a tangible marker of progress and growth. So why judge every step as make or break, put your career in a box, or hide from the challenges that should instead excite your artistry?

There is an ebb and flow to all aspects of existence in-cluding our professional life. When you're in a career slump it can feel interminable. Your inner critic can lead you down a self-defeating spiral of doubt and anxiety, destroying your sense of confidence and ability to perform at your best. You become fearful that you will never succeed, never even have the opportunity to try, be deemed a failure. Don't panic. Don't doubt. Separate work from rewards to keep your perspective true. In a slump you may find yourself reverting back to the self-defeating behaviors and desperate measures that wasted so much creative, emotional and financial capital in the past. Take your eyes off the future, off the enormity of an entire career and focus just on today. What can be done today to further your goals, to break the logjam or bring back the joy of creativity? In a slump, we can begin to take matters personally, discount our own abilities and look to others for solutions. But as an artist you must look to yourself, within yourself, to get back on track.

Examine your personal sense of artistry: have you dis-sipated or corrupted your talent to fit a particular commercial style or project? Have you lost the uniqueness that sets you

171

apart from the crowd? Are you pursuing projects or contacts that don't really interest you or are out of reach at this point in your career? Are you employing teachers, agents, photographers or coaches who are pushing their definitions of success, not yours? If so, stop. Reacquaint yourself with your artistry and your goals. When you subvert that most basic element of your work you are certain to remain in a slump. If you are remaining true to your art, examine your career plan and how well you're putting it into action. Are you really completing all the necessary steps as well as possible? Are you sticking to the plan or drifting, letting weeks and months pass between steps. Is an attitude of defeat or an air of protective distance standing between you and the casting director? These are the behaviors and attitudes that create and sustain slumps. Like all problems, there is a solution. A slump does not have to go on forever or even be wasted time. These are periods when we come to realize the value of our own creativity and the power of our commitment and career plan. That, in itself, is worth the price of a slump. Trust in your talent and be guided by your action plan. Tread water for a while if you have to but stick with what has proven itself to work. Focus on one area of your career for a time and let it be the beneficiary of all your energy. Use this phase to grow your talent. Perhaps now is the time to develop new monologues, review and drill auditions skills or re-edit your voice over demo. Then get out there and put that focused energy back into action. There aren't shortcuts but fulfilling the necessary steps to achieving success with a calm, cool business head allows creativity to flow and progress to follow. Then the clouds part. A booking comes your way and more work follows. You're back in the game because you stayed in the game.

BE AN ASSET NOT A LIABILITY

Problem actors are never worth their talent. Firing someone is expensive and disruptive and not always possible on a tight schedule. Casting directors and producers will play it safe rather than be sorry.

Actors who become the production malcontent are always known to the producers. Their reputation is forever tarnished and other actors usually grouse about that person behind his or her back, even if they encourage the gossip and behavior. If you feel your rights as a union or non-union actor are being violated or your safety is being jeopardized, take appropriate steps to rectify the situation through professional channels. If you have artistic differences, know your place. If you are miserable, respectfully resign.

In this industry, every booking is an audition for your next job. You must build a body of work, including the rehearsal and production periods, which makes you and your talent an asset rather than a liability. During a recent Industry Showcase I hosted, the casting directors on the panel talked about the lack of professionalism they often see in actors called in to audition. When they encounter lateness, a lack of energy and focus, careless appearance and attitude, it sets off alarms. It gives a powerful reason to not hire the actor. Their judgment as casting directors is called into question and that affects the bottom line. Producers and directors need team players. They need to put together a working unit for the duration of the shoot or the run of the show. There isn't time to babysit confused, needy, attention-seeking performers and hold their hands through the job they were hired to do. Once a director or producer views you as a liability who may be poisoning the cast, it is very difficult to reclaim your good professional name.

Always bring your work rather than your personal life to the set or rehearsal. It is the only thing you ever need to bring to the job. When your focus is kept solely on your performance rather than what other actors are doing or not doing, the director's vision or lack thereof or production gossip, you will be an asset. You will be able to look back at your performance and reviews with pride and pleasure. The people who cast, directed and counted on your talent will feel the same way. Actors who work regularly know what a small community this industry really is and that it is easier to succeed with a reputation for stellar acting than one as the source of juicy gossip and toxicity.

AVOID BUSYWORK

Don't get caught in a cycle of busywork. The unpaid gigs few people attend and never get reviewed; the no budget films that are never distributed, the webisodes so poorly conceived and shot they are unwatchable. They do not help your career. It's simply busy work that soothes your ego by making you feel like you're working.

There are always the small budget projects, the labors of love, the interesting risks you are drawn to take. Those are worth doing as are those first few projects that get your career started. It's the busywork that undermines your focus and momentum. The work you do that ends up costing you money, that won't be seen by the industry, never gets reviewed, has no chance of furthering your career in any respect. Many actors spend years toiling in these and then wonder why they are depressed, demoralized and stuck.

When you have your doubts about a role you've been offered, ask yourself if you can afford to do it financially. Can you afford to spend your creative and emotional capital on the project, especially if no one sees it? If the answer is no, politely decline it.

Some ways to gauge if a booking is worth taking is if it will receive quality reviews and press, if it's a stellar vehicle with someone of note attached to the production, if the project has legs that truly benefit you (film distribution or at least a reel or rolls over to a union contract for the regional or pro stage and you get in on the royalty pool). Most people at the developmental level get cut out of backend monies and final credits. Try to find the value in terms of what the job will yield for you as an actor. If the answer is only that it will keep you busy, know that it will cost you in the end. Most actors cannot afford that price.

ACCEPT JOY

You got it! You got the job, the rave review, your commercial is playing nationally and the residual checks are coming in, your agent calls to tell you that producers want to hire you without an audition, the run of the play has just been extended. It's all working just the way you hoped it would and it's making you a nervous wreck. You've struggled for so long and become so used to the grind that the career success you've longed for isn't as enjoyable as you imagined. It feels foreign, unreal. It's a change from what you're used to and that's never easy. What will happen when I the play ends or the residuals dry up? Having a business plan and taking charge of your career means that you are prepared to deal with change, especially good change.

First, enjoy your success, feel secure in the fact that you were hired because you were the right actor for the job and allow that to give wings to your creativity. This is the opportunity to enjoy working and let that joy permeate your performance. Your new co-workers and employers will find your enthusiasm refreshing and want to continue working with you. Because of your career plan you marketed your most castable self so you can be yourself and not feel the need to hide or reinvent. It also means that you have top quality marketing materials and an up-to-date mailing list at your disposal and can publicize your bookings and turn them into more work and recognition. This is the opportunity to target the next level of casting directors or agencies or to use some of that residual income to hire a publicist to get you more press and make a whole new set of industry contacts. When a company produces the new must-have product, they don't sit back and wait for the excitement to end or for the shelves to empty. They build on it. They advertise it more and to new markets because success breeds demand. If you do the same with your success you can keep the flow going and ride this wave to new heights. If you let it scare you, doubt that you deserve it or fail to capitalize on it, success will disappear. An opportunity wasted.

Don't stop being a CEO just when you get to the good stuff because you feel temporarily satisfied or want to rest on your laurels. Renew your commitment to your "company," your career. Seize the moment and climb to the next level. It could be a while before you're back in the salad days again. So savor this time and use it to your best advantage. Make the most of your successes. You've earned it.

Maintain Balance

Strive for balanced expectations between the creative and business aspects of your career and between your career and personal life. The extremes of the early days of your career, the excitement and passion coupled with lack of work and struggle help you to mature as an actor and become more realistic about the business of acting. The slumps and the salad days that follow as you continue as a professional performer teach that careers are cyclical and commitment and clear thinking will see you through the tough times and enhance the good times. But more importantly, taking charge of your acting career, integrating your art throughout your life, allowing yourself to be proud of your talent, your profession, and decision to make it a lifetime pursuit, creates balance within. A whole person, an informed, dedicated professional, a proud member of the cultural community, an Actor.

❏❐❏❐

Acting is a noble professional choice that cannot be achieved by just anyone. A person who creates art that can last for ages, change opinion, move a nation or touch a single soul is a gift to society. It takes talent, originality, intelligence, business acumen, bravery and heart. It means exploring the peaks and valleys so that you can find your creative footing and then exposing this very personal journey to audiences. If you can strive for balance among these myriad aspects, you will be successful. If you can remove doubt and fear, replace it with a career plan, mastery of technique and then allow your unique, balanced artistic self to take flight, you will create your own opportunities. You will have the career of your dreams. You will be a successful actor.

Break a leg.

SUGGESTED READING LIST

This highly selective reading list will give you a broad, working knowledge of Contemporary Theatre from the Greeks through the early 21st Century. The focus of this list is familiarity with seminal roles and styles for actors. This is not a drama lit survey course reading list or a *best of* list. In many cases, I recommend reading plays other than the most well-known by the writer, knowing that you have the option to read them all. This list is all about acting. I've focused on the theatrical rather than film since there are so many sites devoted to viewing lists and books of note in the genre. Theatre, from an acting point of view, is under-represented. Let these suggestions be your starting point.

If your knowledge of acting, technique, social context and performance is spotty or needs refreshing, a number of wonderful reference, critique and historical books are also included on the list

Building your working knowledge of important roles and the writers who create them will add to your ability to deconstruct scripts and make quick, informed choices. Reading these plays and books will immerse you in the art of acting. Enjoy the material, question it, embrace it, try it out for yourself.

Many of the works listed can be found in hard copy in local libraries and for sale in used condition, online at budget friendly prices. Let me know what books you would add to this list. There's no limit!

Reference, Criticism, History & Biography:

The Theatre: A Concise History by Phyllis Hartnoll

The Diaries of Judith Malina by Judith Malina

Up Against the Fourth Wall and any *New Yorker* essays by John Lahr

The Playwright as Thinker: A Study of Drama in Modern Times and *The Life of the Drama* by Eric Bentley

The Theatre of the Absurd by Martin Esslin.

The Empty Space by Peter Brook

An Actor Prepares by Constantin Stanislavski

The Fervent Years: The Group Theatre and the Thirties By Harold Clurman

A Dream of Passion: The Development of the Method by Lee Strasberg

Also suggested: books and articles about designers Adolphe Appia and Gordon Craig. The work of each man had a significant impact on performance in their eras that resonates today.

Plays

Euripides - *Medea, Electra, Trojan Women*

Sophocles - *Oedipus*

Aristophanes - *The Birds*

William Shakespeare - *Macbeth, King Lear, The Merchant of Venice, Julius Caesar, As You Like It, Twelfth Night, King John, The Comedy of Errors, Pericles*

Christopher Marlowe - *Edward the Second, Dido*

Ben Johnson - *Volpone, The Alchemist*

Thomas Middleton - *The Changeling, A Chaste Maid In Cheapside*

Cyril Tourneur - *The Revenger's Tragedy*

Molière - *Tartuffe, The Misanthrope*

Richard Sheridan - *The Rivals, The School for Scandal*

William Congreve - *The Way of the World*

Johann Goethe - *Faust (part one), The Sorrows of Young Werther*

Georg Büchner - *Danton's Death*

Henrik Ibsen - *A Doll's House, Ghosts, Peer Gynt, When We Dead Awaken*

August Strindberg - *Miss Julie, The Father, The Dance of Death*

Oscar Wilde - *The Importance of Being Earnest*

George Bernard Shaw - *Major Barbara, Saint Joan, Arms and the Man*

JM Synge - *The Playboy of the Western World*

Sean O'Casey - *Juno and the Paycock, The Plough and the Stars*

Aleksandr Ostrovsky - *The Storm*

Anton Chekhov - *The Cherry Orchard, Three Sisters, The Seagull*

Federico Garcia Lorca - *Blood Wedding, The House of Bernarda Alba*

Alfred Jarry - *Ubu Roi*

Oskar Kokoschka - *Murder the Women's Hope*

Antonin Artaud - *Jet of Blood*

Tristan Tzara - *The Gas Heart*

Luigi Pirandello - *Six Characters in Search of an Auth*or

Peter Weiss - *Marat/Sade*

Eugene O'Neill - *The Great God Brown, The Hairy Ape, The Emperor Jones, Desire Under the Elms*

Elmer Rice - *The Adding Machine, Street Scene*

William Saroyan - *The Time of Your Life*

Clifford Odets - Awake and Sing, Golden Boy

Maxwell Anderson - Winterset

Sidney Kingsley - *Dead End*

Thornton Wilder - *Our Town, The Skin of Our Teeth*

Lillian Hellman - The Little Foxes, The Children's Hour

Tennessee Williams - *A Streetcar Named Desire, The Glass Menagerie*

Arthur Miller - *Death of a Salesman, A View from the Bridge*

Samuel Beckett - *Waiting for Godot, Happy Days*

Bertolt Brecht - *Mother Courage, The Caucasian Chalk Circle*

Friedrich Dürrenmatt - *The Visit*
Eugène Ionesco - *The Chairs, Rhinoceros*
John Osborne - *Look Back in Anger*
William Inge - *Picnic, Come Back Little Sheba*
Joe Orton - *Entertaining Mr. Sloane, Loot*
Lorraine Hansberry - *A Raisin in the Sun*
Harold Pinter - *The Homecoming, The Birthday Party*
Tom Stoppard - *Arcadia, The Real Thing*
Jean Genet - *The Balcony*
David Mamet - *American Buffalo, Glengarry Glen Ross*
Athol Fugard -*Sizwe Bansi Is Dead, Master Harold . . . and the Boys*
Amiri Baraka - *Dutchman and the Slaves*
Arthur Kopit - *Oh Dad, Poor Dad, Mamma's Hung You in the Closet and I'm Feeling So Sad*
Ntozke Shange - *For Colored Girls Who Have Considered Suicide When the Rainbow is Enuf*
August Wilson - *Fences*
Caryl Churchill - *Top Girls, Serious Money*
Marsha Norman - *'night Mother*
Wendy Wasserstein - *Uncommon Women and Others, The Heidi Chronicles*
Christopher Durang - *Sister Mary Ignatius Explains It All to You*
Beth Henley - *Crimes of the Heart*
John Guare - *Six Degrees of Separation*
Jane Martin - *Talking With . . .*
Tina Howe - *Museum*
Craig Lucas - *Prelude to a Kiss*
Theresa Rebeck - *Loose Knit, Seminar*
Romulus Linney - *Holy Ghosts*
Lee Blessing - *Independence*
Sherry Kramer - *David's RedHaired Death*
David Hare - *Skylight, The Secret Rapture*
Brian Friel -*Dancing at Lughnasa*
Jane Anderson - *Food and Shelter*
Naomi Iizuka - *Aloha, Say the Pretty Girls*

Suzan-Lori Parks - *Topdog/Underdog, Venus*
Keith Bunin - *The Busy World is Hushed*
Sharr White - *Six Years*
John Patrick Shanley - Doubt
Martin McDonagh - *The Lieutenant of Inishmore, The Beauty Queen of Leenane*
Adam Rapp - *Red* Light Winter
Rebecca Gilman - *Boy Meets Girl*
Nicky Silver - *The Maiden's Prayer*
Yasmina Reza - *Art*
Tracy Letts - *August: Osage County*
Sarah Ruhl - *The Clean House*
Lloyd Suh - *American Hwangap*

The most cost effective way to read a cross section of new works is through the many collections of work from festivals and theatre companies. Rather than citing specific works, I will cite some of my favorite collections, many of which are released with new material annually.

The Humana Festival Collections (published by Smith and Kraus)
Women Playwrights: The Best of (year) . . . (published by Smith and Kraus)
*The Best Plays of (*year) Published by Smith and Kraus
Colored Contradictions - Elam and Alexander.
And, Smith and Kraus' annual anthologies of *Best Stage Monologues and Scenes* are an excellent source for audition material.

ABOUT THE AUTHOR

Cynthia White has coached professional actors and acting students all over the country and world through her company, IndependentActor NYC. A 2002 recipient of the New York Foundation for the Arts Artist Award, her work as an actor, director and writer encompasses stage, screen and new media. Her voice can be heard on numerous television and radio commercials, animation and video games.